REFERENCE GUIDES TO RHETORIC AND COMPOSITION

Series Editor, Charles Bazerman

REFERENCE GUIDES TO RHETORIC AND COMPOSITION
Series Editor, Charles Bazerman

The Series provides compact, comprehensive and convenient surveys of what has been learned through research and practice as composition has emerged as an academic discipline over the last half century. Each volume is devoted to a single topic that has been of interest in rhetoric and composition in recent years, to synthesize and make available the sum and parts of what has been learned on that topic. These reference guides are designed to help deepen classroom practice by making available the collective wisdom of the field and will provide the basis for new research. The Series is intended to be of use to teachers at all levels of education, researchers and scholars of writing, graduate students learning about the field, and all who have interest in or responsibility for writing programs and the teaching of writing.

Parlor Press and The WAC Clearinghouse are collaborating so that these books will be widely available through low-cost print editions and free digital distribution. The publishers and the Series editor are teachers and researchers of writing, committed to the principle that knowledge should freely circulate. We see the opportunities that new technologies have for further democratizing knowledge. And we see that to share the power of writing is to share the means for all to articulate their needs, interest, and learning into the great experiment of literacy.

Reference Guide to
Writing Across the Curriculum

Reference Guide to Writing Across the Curriculum

Charles Bazerman, Joseph Little, Lisa Bethel, Teri Chavkin, Danielle Fouquette, and Janet Garufis

Parlor Press
West Lafayette, Indiana
www.parlorpress.com

The WAC Clearinghouse
http://wac.colostate.edu/

Parlor Press LLC, West Lafayette, Indiana 47906

© 2005 by Parlor Press and The WAC Clearinghouse
All rights reserved.
Printed in the United States of America

S A N: 2 5 4 - 8 8 7 9

Library of Congress Cataloging-in-Publication Data

Reference guide to writing across the curriculum / Charles Bazerman
... [et al.].
      p. cm. -- (Reference guides to rhetoric and composition)
   Includes bibliographical references and index.
   ISBN 1-932559-42-6 (pbk. : alk. paper) -- ISBN 1-932559-43-4 (hard-
cover : alk. paper) -- ISBN 1-932559-44-2 (Adobe ebook) 1. Language
arts--Correlation with content subjects. 2. Interdisciplinary approach in
education--History. I. Bazerman, Charles. II. Series.
   LB1576.R435 2005
   808'.042'071--dc22
                                           2005009596

Series logo designed by Karl Stolley.
This book is printed on acid-free paper.

Parlor Press, LLC is an independent publisher of scholarly and trade titles in
print and multimedia formats. This book is also available in cloth and Adobe
eBook formats from Parlor Press on the World Wide Web at http://www.
parlorpress.com. For submission information or to find out about Parlor Press
publications, write to Parlor Press, 816 Robinson St., West Lafayette, Indiana,
47906, or e-mail editor@parlorpress.com.

The WAC Clearinghouse supports teachers of writing across the disciplines.
Hosted by Colorado State University's Composition Program, it brings together four journals, three book series, and resources for teachers who use
writing in their courses. This book will also be available free on the Internet at
The WAC Clearinghouse (http://wac.colostate.edu/).

Contents

Preface

In editing this series of Reference Guides to Rhetoric and Composition I have been motivated by the need for the field of composition to synthesize the work of the last several decades of its professionalization. I have also wanted to gather the perspectives of people who have been deeply engaged in building this practical and research knowledge in each of its subfields to assess what we have learned.

I arrived in the profession via the City University of New York during the early years of the pioneering Open Admissions Policy, a few years before the first murmurings about Writing Across the Curriculum. This policy put the issue of what writing skills were necessary for college success front and center to those teaching writing. The nontraditional students we taught were frequently basic writers, and we needed to help them develop quickly and in a focused manner sufficient writing competence to deal with the demands of higher education. What that competence was, however, was under-defined and under-studied. There was virtually no understanding of what, if anything, distinguished academic writing from other forms of writing, particularly literary writing and popular journalism. A number of us, urged by Mina Shaughnessy, started probing this issue.

When we first caught wind of the writing across the curriculum movement being born in other regions, we immediately saw the great value of this. I remember a contingent of us heading down the New Jersey Turnpike in Spring of 1978 to the Delaware Valley Writing Conference with the theme of Writing Across the Curriculum run by Elaine Maimon at Beaver College, just outside Philadelphia. From my perspective, this seemed exactly what we needed to begin to understand what academic writing was, how it varied across disciplines, and how work in various disciplines supported the development of academic writing or penalized the lack of it. While WAC had great force as a programmatic and practical endeavor, it also created the need for research into writing in the disciplines at both a professional and classroom level.

Over a quarter of a century later, we have learned much about writing across the curriculum and the associated disciplines and professions. We also have learned much about how to grow and run successful WAC programs in different campus cultures. This book draws the history of the movement together with the research and programmatic savvy we have developed. I hope the synthesis here will help us make sense of where we have been and where we are heading. Working with my coauthors Joe Little, Lisa Bethel, Teri Chavkin, Danielle Fouquette, and Janet Garufis, who were viewing this material with a fresh eye, I have come to appreciate much more all that has been accomplished in this period. We would also like to thank Susan McLeod, Michael Palmquist, and David Russell for their careful reading of the manuscript and helpful suggestions.

We hope this reference and synthesis will spur a new generation of research, theory, and program development. We are now starting to understand the writing challenges students face in their educations and how programmatic support can be offered to help them meet these challenges, but we need to know much more and at all levels of education, from the primary years through graduate school.

—*Charles Bazerman*

Reference Guide to
Writing Across the Curriculum

Part I. The WAC Movement

1

Introduction to Key Concepts

Writing Across the Curriculum, like any academic program, arises out of a complex of institutional, intellectual, and social events and forces. The complex set of impulses, goals, and endeavors set forth by those events and forces have varying names and configurations. So before venturing into the detailed examination of programs and knowledge, it is useful to sort out some of the common terms used to describe educational programs. The definitions, in themselves, will begin to set out a larger historical, institutional, and intellectual picture to be filled in by the chapters that follow. The terms will be arranged in three clusters. The first cluster presents terms identifying the relations between literacy and schooling in historical and institutional contexts. The second cluster presents terms identifying ways of organizing writing and reading curricula with respect to other subject areas. The final cluster defines two terms central to thinking about the use of reading in academic writing.

Literacy and Schooling

The practices and development of writing and reading have been intimately tied to the histories of schooling. Indeed, literacy education has been the primary motivation for developing most educational institutions throughout history—that is, places of organized instruction apart from the daily flow and interaction of life practices. People in daily life are constantly learning from the people around them and the tasks they face, but institutions of schooling set up activities that are to some degree separated from the activities of daily life. Reading and writing take one out of the flow of events and immediate activities, requiring some retreat to attend to words that somehow extend beyond the current moment. Reading and writing are not easily taught in passing, but require extended concentration away from other concerns, particularly in relation to the more complex and contemplative functions of literacy we have developed.

Reading and Writing Activities in Schooling

As social needs for literacy increased, so did schooling. Further, the reading and writing activities in school were often closely tied to the specific social functions that created the need for advanced literacy. Scriptural religions created the need for high degrees of literacy in the priestly castes and in some cases placed a literacy obligation on all believers. In schools associated with all the major religions, the primary reading matter and writing practices were associated with the scriptures and other religious obligations.

Insofar as literacy was driven by the needs of bureaucracies or commerce, these also then provided the matter and motive for literacy education. Even whether handwriting was taught and which style of script was practiced depended on the role students would take on in the economy. In America writing was first associated with commerce and handwriting particularly associated with business and administrative activities (Thornton, 1996). Women were taught to read, but since they did not engage in commerce, they were not taught handwriting, but instead needlepoint (Monaghan, 1989).

Literacy in the Rhetorical University

In mid-nineteenth century higher education in the U.S., literacy was tied to social, governmental, and religious leadership. The matter and motive of literacy education were therefore shaped around theology, homiletics, philosophy, government, and rhetoric within a largely integrated curriculum.

Literacy in the Research University

With the rise of the departmental research university in the later nineteenth century, however, the relationship between writing and subject matters changed. First, the various subject matters were separated from language and rhetorical study. Although one might continue to read and write within moral philosophy or biology or history, there was little instruction or focus on the writing, which was viewed simply as the vehicle of disciplinary communication. Writing was taken for granted, and when students had difficulty with the literacy assignments it was viewed as a fault of their language instruction or the weakness of the students themselves. Second, the department gaining authority over literacy instruction was philology and literary studies, so that literacy instruction was placed in the service of and under the values and practices of literary studies.

Literacy in High Schools

The departmental arrangement of university education and the location of literacy instruction within departments of literature influenced literacy instruction in the modern high school. High schools emerged largely as a means of college preparation, though in the late nineteenth century and first half of the twentieth century only a small percentage of high school students went on to college (Tanner & Tanner, 1990). As a preparation for college, high schools, adopted the departmental divisions of the university and framed their curricula along the lines of the university courses. Thus language arts in the secondary schools were taught in the English class, whose definition of language was taken from literary studies.

Academic Literacy

Academic Literacy is a term that combines reading and writing. This is appropriate in that reading and writing never occur separately, but are always part of a shared field of activity. In the academic disciplines professionals students read and they write. They write about and use what they read (see definition of "intertextuality" below). And their writing forms the reading of their teachers, colleagues, and students. The term academic literacy is most widely used in reference to the lower and middle grades of schooling, to distinguish the kinds of reading and writing students are expected to do in school from the kinds of reading and writing children might do in their daily life outside of school. Sometimes, most narrowly, the term (or its close relation Academic English) is used to refer to conventions of language correctness that students are expected to adhere to in school. This narrowing of the term is unfortunate. While children in school are often monitored for adherence to formal language conventions, academic literacy embodies a much wider range of practices, skills, and interactions that bring students into intellectual engagement with knowledge, thought, and the work of professions.

Academic Language Socialization

Academic language socialization is the process by which individuals learn to enter into the discussions and again access to the resources of academic disciplines through learning specialized language use and participating in academic activity settings. Learning to read and write in academic settings occurs through extended experiences in those settings, by meeting the expectations of those situations, and gaining from the opportunities for participation they offer.

Literacy and Curriculum

The assignment of reading and writing, though a necessary vehicle for the study of the various subjects, remained in the background as practices, receiving little instruction outside English and language arts classrooms. If students were unable to complete the reading and writing, or were otherwise found wanting the instructors often separated subject matter knowledge and competence from the language competence—thus marking the history part of the essay or intuiting what the student meant to say rather than holding them accountable for their precise articulation of the subject matter in writing. Failures in reading or writing in the subject matter might be penalized or might be gotten around through alternative instructional strategies, but they were not seen as matters for instruction within the context of the subject area.

These separations of literacy from content knowledge, here drawn with wide brush-strokes, set the stage for a re-engagement between literacy education and the particular subject matters, but only after the teaching of writing gained some degree of independence from the literary curriculum. This happened in the 1970s as the field of composition began to gather some professional authority and was able to assert some of its educational objectives apart from the literary curriculum. As literacy started to be understood more fully as distinct from literary education and the tacit reading and writing components of the school and university curriculum became recognized more explicitly, several related pedagogical movements arose. They are closely related but are somewhat distinct, as will be spelled out in later chapters. We can, here, however, associate specific terms with distinctive aspects of this movement.

First-Year Writing (or Composition

Insofar as writing was explicitly taught within the research university it was typically taught in a first year course meant to prepare students for the writing demands of the university. This course often had a remedial or transitional character, so that students who were not writing well enough to meet the requirements of their other courses would be given developmental writing experiences. First year courses were frequently supplemented by even more basic writing courses, with placement determined by an examination at the time of entry into the university. These courses were typically staffed by junior faculty, lecturers, and graduate students, usually affiliated with the English Department.

Writing Across the Curriculum

Writing Across the Curriculum (WAC) refers specifically to the pedagogical and curricular attention to writing occurring in university subject matter classes other than those offered by composition or writing programs (most often housed in the English Department). The movement provided systematic encouragement, institutional support, and educational knowledge to increase the amount and quality of writing occurring in such courses as history, science, mathematics and sociology. As will be spelled out in this volume, there have been many approaches to the kinds of writing encouraged, the kind of support offered, and the knowledge thought useful to student and teacher—but they were all directed to classrooms other than the writing or composition classes.

Writing in the Disciplines

Writing in the Disciplines (WID), although often associated with Writing Across the Curriculum, is distinct from WAC. WID refers to both a research movement to understand what writing actually occurs in the different disciplinary areas and a curricular reform movement to offer disciplinary related writing instruction but within a program designed for that purpose (whether university-wide or departmentally located).

The research within the WID movement is based on the awareness that prior assumptions we had about what constituted good writing and what writing should be taught were based on literary models. In order to support writing across the curriculum intelligently we needed to know what kind of writing actually got done in the disciplines by professionals, how it got done, and what aspects of the writing were most highly valued. We needed, additionally, to understand better the writing that occurred within disciplinary classes, for it could not be assumed to be the same as that done by professionals. We need to understand the differences, similarities, and relationship between them to provide wise guidance for teachers and students writing within their disciplines.

The curricular movement is then to provide discipline-specific support for writing instruction and learning through writing. Often this is offered in upper division courses for students already committed to majors. Thus students might have the option of taking one of a series of courses with titles such as writing for sociology, writing for the biological sciences, writing for history, writing for business and economics, and so on. These courses would be offered usually within the writing or English programs by writing specialists who had developed particular expertise in the area. Sometimes, they would be offered within the different disciplinary departments. In some cases the first year writing course would take a writing in the disciplines approach, by offering students a survey of the kinds of writing they would encounter in the university.

Writing-Intensive or Writing-Emphasis Courses

In conjunction with a WAC or WID program, students may be required to take a set number of courses that require a minimum amount of writing and perhaps offer task specific writing support and instruction. Such courses are designated by such titles as writing intensive, writing emphasis, or writing requirement courses.

Writing in the Professions

Writing in the Professions is a parallel research and curricular movement directed towards professions that carried on their work largely outside the university, such as the medical professions, law, and engineering. This movement overlaps with business and technical writing. A separate volume in this series will be devoted to Writing in the Professions. Writing in the Workplace is a similar research and curricular program associated with adult literacy programs.

Writing in Content Areas

Writing in Content Areas is sometimes used to describe Writing Across the Curriculum initiatives in high schools or occasionally primary schools. The use of the term content or subject area rather than curriculum suggests how secondary and primary study areas are less loosely tied to academic disciplines than in the university. Curriculum is defined as subject matters or content, packaged for classroom transmission, rather than disciplinary practices. The social spaces of the different subject classrooms within a school define the realm of activity rather than the nationally or internationally structured disciplines of knowledge.

Reading

The major terms concerning literacy within disciplinary contexts in relation to higher education have been cast in terms of writing. Writing Across the Curriculum practice and Writing in the Disciplines research have regularly run into the fact that most academic writing is closely tied to reading and regularly references reading. Often academic writing assignments specifically require particular use to be made of reading, such as summary or response. However, there has developed no substantial movement in higher education designated by the term reading across the curriculum. Nor has there been much formal programmatic support for reading in relation to particular disciplinary curricular areas in higher education. Further there has been only limited research into the uses of reading in writing or professional disciplinary reading practices, which will be discussed in following sections. The research on reading in disciplinary contexts is largely from the point of view of writing, that is, how a writer deploys and cites their source texts in their writing. Thus the focus of this research is intertextuality (defined below), though there are some studies focused specifically on reading practices.

Reading in Content Areas

Reading in Content Areas or Reading in the Subject Areas is a term used in relation to K-12 schooling, with particular reference to the kinds of reading practices need within primary and secondary classrooms. Thus there is a heavy emphasis on textbook reading, focussing attention on such skills as information extraction, main idea identification, and inferential reasoning. The field devotes little attention to other disciplinary reading activities or the use of the reading in a variety of writing settings.

Writing Using Reading

Intertextuality

Intertextuality is the way in which one piece of writing refers to, invokes, relies on, echoes, or otherwise uses other pieces of writing. The most explicit and direct form of intertextuality is direct quotation and citation. Paraphrase, summary, and mention of another's idea with or without formal reference to another text form a spectrum, which has as its other extreme the use of phrases and forms that echo earlier texts with no explicit mention. Because academic knowledge building and use is a collective enterprise, building on the ideas, research, and applications of prior researchers and responding to the proposals and arguments of contemporary others, intertextuality is a major visible phenomenon in academic writing. However, since all our language use responds to what others have said previously and draws on resources they have provided, all language can be said to be intertextual. See Chapter 7 for further elaboration.

Plagiarism

Plagiarism is the use of intertextual resources without giving adequate identification to the origin of those resources. However, we cannot and are not expected to give credit to the first place we heard every idea, fact, word, phrase, or rhetorical form. Only on some occasions are we expected to credit some particular sources in some particular formats. The transgression characterized as plagiarism marks the conventional and situational boundaries identifying what part of that intertextuality needs to be explicitly recognized and where explicit credit needs to be given to prior authors and texts. That is, plagiarism is the failure to identify the words of others through marking of quotations or the source of ideas and information in those situations where such identification is currently expected.

Plagiarism is a recurrently important issue in academic and disciplinary writing for several reasons. First, professional credit and rewards are distributed to academics and other researchers and professionals on the basis of their discoveries, inventions, and other contributions presented in their publications. Not mentioning the sources of disciplinarily important contributions both denies credit to the innovator and appears to present the innovation as coming from the new author.

Second, students are expected in their assignments to demonstrate some degree of originality and thought based upon the knowledge and ideas of others. This expectation is both to encourage intellectual work for students and to assess their accomplishments. Not giving credit to sources allows students to take credit for the work of others and, even more, to evade the responsibility for doing serious intellectual work. If, for example, however, the entire class is answering questions based on a single textbook used by the entire class, the teacher has no difficulty in sorting out what is from the book and what is the students' work, so there is often no need for regular citation practices. In schooling citation and plagiarism are usually much more of an issue when the students are drawing on a range of sources that they have obtained on their own from beyond the shared work of the classroom.

Finally, the quality of both student and professional work depends on the quality of the work of others that they draw on. Not citing the sources of academic knowledge and thought leaves the writer without the authority of the prior work and leaves the reader without clues about how to assess the quality and contribution of the new work. These reasons for concern about plagiarism in the academy are somewhat different than those reasons that pertain to the marketplace, having to do with the economic value of intellectual property. Thus rules of plagiarism in commercial law are significantly different than those in the academy. Copyright, rather than recognition of intellectual resources, forms the center of the commercial legal definition of plagiarism.

2

History of the WAC Movement

American Roots of Writing Across the Curriculum to 1970

The set of conditions in United States' universities that gave rise to the Writing Across the Curriculum Movement in the latter part of the twentieth century arose out of a much longer history of secondary and higher education in the United States. That history resulted in a specialized undergraduate curriculum and the isolation of literacy and rhetorical instruction from the rest of the curriculum.

Prior to the late 19th century, a four-year college education was primarily rhetorical and was directed toward the production of a religious and secular elite. College education aimed to create leaders who could speak eloquently and articulately from the pulpit, in the chambers of government, or among the leaders of commerce. The subject matter and professional training offered by the colleges of the colonies and early republic were closely associated with the forms of public presentation that the students learned to master and that marked their achievement. The education was comprised largely of making oral recitations and studying principles of rhetoric in a liberal arts curriculum as preparation for careers in law, medicine, or theology (Adams, 1993). However, college was not a necessary precursor for employment. Both future lawyers and doctors could certainly attend college lectures in politics, government, or ethics but their practical training happened through apprenticeship. Thus higher education was as much a marker of class as of specific career training.

Two events, however, marked major turning points in the nature of college education. First, the passage of the Morrill Act of 1862 defined a new mission for higher education. The act established the agricultural and mechanical colleges, making new kinds of careers available for college study and altering the college curriculum at many schools (Brereton, 1995, p. 9). "By 1900," writes Adams, "at the more than 750 universities, colleges, and technical institutes across the country, students generally took liberal arts courses in their first two years and then chose among tracks in engineering, agriculture, education, library science, business home economics, the humanities, and other fields [...] [for] the last two years" (Adams, 1993, p. 1). Second, the opening of Johns Hopkins University in 1876 indicated a turn toward the German research university as a model of higher education. The research university brought with it specialization of departments, directed towards the faculty production of new knowledge in distinct domains, and the training of students to become researchers and specialists. These disciplines each developed its own specialized form of language, but had no place within its curriculum for disciplinary language training, rhetoric or writing. Indeed no field had at first focused responsibility for these areas, for even English Departments found their research focus in philology and literary studies. Rather competence in literacy and communication was assumed at the student's entry into the specialty, as it still is currently in many European universities that also adopted the German research model.

However, the specialization of the research university came in conflict with the democratization and increased accessibility of the university, leading to renewed interest in literacy education at the university. As student enrollments began increasing around the 1870s, these students were deemed deficient in writing skills, particularly mechanics and correctness of writing (Connors, 1991), and parents, professors, and the general public grew anxious over this presumed deficiency. Harvard responded to this increased public concern over literacy and linguistic correctness by implementing college entrance exams in written English in 1874. In the first year, over half the students failed the exams and people questioned how students who hailed from the best secondary schools could not write correctly. Several other colleges began administering similar entrance exams and before long the Harvard examiners and other academics soon began to push for "better training on the secondary level and for more effective writing instruction on the college level" (Connors, 1991, p. 4). In short, the mandatory freshman year composition course was created in response to the literacy crisis of 1875–1885. However, while principles of argumentation, exposition, logic—tools of the classical rhetorician's trade—were a necessary part of the pre-modern American university, practice in these areas was relegated to a single composition course at the beginning of the student's college career at the turn of the 20th century. This course separated writing from the subject matters and career orientation pursued by students, and aimed at developing general writing skills based on a model of general cognitive faculties (Adams, 1993).

Concerns for the preparation of students for the university also led to reform of the nation's secondary schools. Secondary schools had been since their inception directed towards college preparation. At first, when colleges offered rhetorical education for the elites, Latin grammar schools were the most common form of the secondary school (Tanner & Tanner, 1990). These gradually were supplemented by more practically oriented private academies, but not until high schools were formed in the last decades of the nineteenth century was there a major change in secondary education. The public high schools were community based and had more open access. They offered electives fitting the interests and career goals of students within a contemporary world. Nonetheless, the curriculum was shaped by college entrance requirements, even though in 1890 only about 15 percent of high school students were preparing for college. The disciplinary-focused college preparation curriculum was cemented by the so-called Committee of Ten, organized by the National Education Association. This influential committee, which included five college presidents and was chaired by President of Harvard Charles W. Eliot, recommended in 1893 a high school curriculum based on nine subjects that directly corresponded to and prepared students for university courses: Latin, Greek, English (literature, composition, grammar), other modern languages, mathematics, physical sciences, natural history (biology), history and government, and geography. This curriculum reinforced the effect of the disciplinary research university on writing, pushing down into secondary education the same pattern of writing taught only as part of a literary-dominated English curriculum.

The logic of this disciplinary organization of universities and secondary schools located responsibility for writing instruction within a single discipline of English that found its higher aspirations in literature rather than student writing. Nonetheless, a "cooperation movement" attempted in the opening decades of the twentieth century to enlist the teachers of all subjects into the teaching of writing (Russell, 1991). But this movement was difficult to maintain in the face of the increasing specialization of secondary and university departments and the management of educational institutions for efficiency through specialization and bureaucratization. The cooperation movement diminished with WWII, but did survive at the margins, along with other progressive educational ideas.

While writing instruction for students in general became restricted in scope and subordinated to a literary curriculum, some specialized forms of writing developed niche presences. Creative writing had become a widely offered university course by the early twentieth century, as did journalistic writing (Adams, 1993). In both cases a number of career-focused degree programs had developed by mid-twentieth century. Two other kinds of specialized writing courses also developed around the turn of the twentieth century to meet the special needs of students in engineering and business degrees, often instigated by complaints of employers. Although such courses were originally taught within English departments, as the courses became increasingly specialized in character there was a tendency for the courses to be offered through the professional school (Russell, 1991). Even today the pattern remains mixed, with technical writing sometimes being taught by a program in technical writing located in the engineering school and sometimes located in the English department. A similar diversity of arrangements has developed for business writing. Nonetheless, in both cases, the courses were designed and offered for the needs of a particular group of professional students, coordinated with their professional training. Students outside those professional programs were not expected to enroll in these specialized writing courses. These courses and programs also developed practices, beliefs, and goals that for the most part became quite distinct from those of composition.

Between 1920 and 1930 enrollments at American universities nearly doubled from 598,000 students to over one million, and the mandatory college course—freshman composition—became both highly visible and the target of attack (Connors, 1995). At the 1931 National Council of Teachers in English (NCTE) meeting, Alvin C. Eurich shared findings from a late 1920s study conducted at his university, the University of Minnesota (Eurich, 1932). Essays collected from 54

freshmen both before and after completing their freshman composition course at Minnesota were reviewed using one of several popular
essay rating scales. The essays revealed that no significant improvement was made over the course of three months. The conclusions
drawn from Eurich's scholarly research report were that extended habits of written expression cannot be influenced in such a short time, and
he advocated one of the earlier forms of WAC where English teachers
and those in other fields would collaborate to design writing-based assignments. This early push towards WAC was fervently discussed but
not taken up seriously until several decades later. Yet spirited debates
regarding the usefulness of a term-length composition course—essentially the heart of Eurich's conclusions—did ensue. One of those debates carrying additional WAC undertones was sparked by the 1935
NCTE Committee on College English's *The Teaching of College English,* which decried the freshman year composition model and advocated moving it to the sophomore year instead. The *English Journal*
published all the arguments and ripostes on the topic in one of their
sections titled "Symposium." Oscar J. Campbell, chair of the Symposium committee, posited an implicit writing across the curriculum
message himself when he remarked:

> What your students need is not more instruction in
> writing but a few teachers of geology who are capable
> of describing not only geological phenomena but also
> of teaching their students how to think consecutively
> and logically about geology [...]. Since most teach-
> ers of geology, history, or economics find themselves
> incapable of it, they conceal their incompetence from
> themselves by shifting the responsibility of their fail-
> ure upon the harried instructor in Freshman English,
> who labors valiantly to accomplish the impossible.
> (Campbell, 1939, p. 181)

However, his intentionally inflammatory comments had little effect as
World War II tabled discussions about the value of freshman composition. (For further discussion of this debate, see Russell, 1988.)

In the post-war years, tremendous changes in secondary and postsecondary education occurred in America. The returning solders attending college on the GI Bill were the leading edge of an expansion,
democratization, and diversity of higher education. In the ensuing de-

cades, race, class, and gender became less and less barriers to enroll-
ment at increasingly large numbers of institutions. At the same time
technology soared and federal and corporate research funding led to
a "knowledge explosion" at colleges and universities as well as in the
workplace. Completing a secondary education became a minimum requirement for success in life. A college education began to resonate
with more and more Americans and many viewed it as an attainable
necessity. Thus, as more people raised the bar of success for themselves
and society, a new quest for literacy excellence began and with it increased scrutiny on writing quality. "Americans learned that poor writing was a serious problem, from the high-school dropout to the Ph.D.
candidate," says Russell. And "[i]ncreasing specialization in education
and in work demanded that students be taught to write for a host of
new situations" (Russell, 1991, p. 240). A call to improve the quality of
writing was sounded and the communications movement of the post-
war era took up this cause.

The communications movement originated "from a new interest in
semantics and scientific study of communication and the mobilization
of American education for the war effort and postwar adjustment"
(Russell, 1991, p. 256). While it did not do much to alter writing
pedagogy, it did begin to move the onus of teaching writing to disciplines outside of English and literary study. This shift was largely
accomplished by the theoretical backing of I. A. Richards' *The Philosophy of Rhetoric* (1936) where he proposed a "transformed discipline
of rhetoric [that] would study all types of discourse as *functions* of linguistics behavior" (Russell, 1991, p. 257). Richards's efforts to modify
language instruction resulted in the Progressive Education Association
releasing a report connecting "the development of language skill with
learning in all disciplines" (p. 257) and associating language facili-
ty with critical thinking. The linkage of language to critical thought
soon extended to the linkage of language and disciplinary modes of
thought. The four areas intricately tied to language development—listening, speaking, reading, and writing—were given renewed status
as foundational in many disciplines. The communications movement
laid "the groundwork for a revival [...] in rhetoric in the 1960s, which
in turn led to the WAC movement in the 1970s" (Russell, 1991, p.
256–257).

The social and political forces at work in the 1960s, including racial integration in mass education, exposed the divisions in school

language policy and the need to teach the dominant language to excluded populations. Composition theorists such as Peter Elbow, Ken Macrorie, Donald Graves, and James Moffett were making their presence known with their Deweyian emphasis on classroom communities and student-centered teaching. While Jerome S. Bruner's (1963, 1964, 1986) important research on the effects of language in all disciplines would take some time to be widely disseminated, his focus on disciplinary rigor quickly drew considerable attention (Bazerman & Russell, 1994). On the surface, although his discipline-centered approach seemed a stark contrast to the student-centered one posited by some of the composition expressivists noted above, it was largely influenced by Jean Piaget and Dewey and focused on student development and progress.

The renewed interest in communication, rhetoric, and writing in the U.S. in the 1960s manifested itself in the rise of composition studies as an academic discipline, replete with its own books, journals and scholarly methods (Connors, 1995). The formation of this discipline offered a new academic forum for experimentation in writing instruction and pedagogy, and the professionals drawn to this field, though usually situated in English departments, were more interdisciplinary by professional nature, further opening the door to writing across the curriculum theories.

The Influence of British Reforms in the 1960s and 1970s

While the structure, growth, and demographics of the American university set the stage for the Writing Across the Curriculum movement, it was educational reform coming from Britain that provided the catalyst and sources for the movement. Curricular developments and research fostered by James Britton and his colleagues at the London School of Education from 1966–1976, in particular seeded the WAC movement (Russell, 1991; Bazerman & Russell, 1994). Britton's work was first introduced to American educators at a 1966 Dartmouth Seminar (Dixon, 1967). Composition was only marginally addressed at the conference; the main focus was on pedagogical reform and student liberation. However, several British conference participants, James Britton, Douglas Barnes, and Harold Rosen, soon became key figures in the WAC movement.

In an instance of educational irony, the British approach to education broadly paralleled the American progressive tradition of the 1920s
and 1930s posited by Dewey and emphasizing "experience-centered
awareness" (Russell, 1994, p. 11). In the U.S., however, this approach
had been largely abandoned since WWII in favor of a pedagogy more
focused on disciplinary rigor, general curricula, and objective evaluation. American NCTE leaders at the 1966 Dartmouth Seminar were
harshly criticized by their British counterparts (NATE) for sticking
to overly rigid models of writing, language, and literary instruction.
Concerned with the linguistic, social, and personal development of
the student, the British favored a looser form of classroom talk and
privileged students' personal responses. The British critique resonated
sharply with American reformers, and the States soon imported British language and writing theories into their curriculum.

While the WAC movement in America was to focus mainly on reform in higher education, British efforts targeted secondary education
(Russell, 1994). In 1972, Britain's national education commission—as
it was periodically requested to do—investigated the current educational crisis created by the demand for increased access to secondary
schools and colleges, similar to the challenges open admissions policies
had created in the States. The commission was given the hefty task of
investigating everything they could find related to teaching English.
They did so and three years later issued their 600-page investigative
report. In it they noted the difficulty involved in determining whether
written and spoken standards of English had actually slipped. They
focused instead on the higher standards demanded by the changing
workplace and higher education and determined it was these higher
standards and the subsequent exposure that led to the cries of communication "deficiencies" (Russell, 1991, p. 277). The commission
proposed curriculum reform that advocated "informal classroom
talk, especially in small groups; expressive writing; and teacher-stu-
dent collaboration" (Russell, 1991, p. 277). As a commission member,
James Britton played an influential role. His 1970 book, *Language and
Learning,* which argued that language is central to learning, figured
significantly in the commission's recommendations (see also Barnes,
Britton, & Rosen, 1970). Later, he served as the main contributor to
The Bullock Report's chapter on "Language Across the Curriculum,"
where language was noted to play an important role in discipline-specific learning (Bullock, 1975). The chapter called for writing in all

classes, not just English classes—the title phrase made its way across the Atlantic and was transformed into Writing Across the Curriculum, or WAC, in the U.S.

One of the most influential studies coming out of the British writing-across-the-curriculum research and later informing the American WAC movement was another project spearheaded by Britton. At the behest of the Schools Councils Project, a high-level advisory group comprised of business, government, and educational leaders (Russell, 1991, p. 279), Britton and his colleagues conducted a detailed survey of student writing in British schools. At the center of their landmark study was Britton's theory "that children develop writing ability by moving from personal forms of writing (what he calls *expressive* and *poetic*) to more public, workaday forms, which communicate information (what he calls *transactional*)" (Russell, 1991, p. 278). The study found that most writing in British schools was transactional with children receiving very few opportunities to write in the expressive or poetic style and consequently very few chances to develop their writing abilities organically. On the basis of this study reported in Britton, Burgess, Martin, McLeod, and Rosen's 1975 book *The Development of Writing Abilities,* the Schools Council Project recommended a complete curricular change to redress the lack of expressive writing in schools. Works coming out of that initiative include Marland (1977), Martin (1976), and Martin (1984). These British theories were the American educators' antidote to the formalist/cognitivist writing pedagogy in place for several decades, where correctness of form was associated with the development of intellectual habits and abilities. American compositionists embraced both the expressivist pedagogy and the project's name, writing across the curriculum.

Workshops, National Organizations and Dissemination

How did word spread about this new idea that came to be known as Writing Across the Curriculum? A progressively more aggressive campaign to move writing out of the exclusive domain of the English department is documented in professional journals:

> 1939: "The Failure of English Composition" *English Journal* (Campbell)

1949: "Faculty Responsibility for Student Writing" *College English* (Wright)

1960: "College Wide English Improvement" *College English* (McCullogh)

1967: "English Does Not Belong to the English Class" *English Journal* (Kaufman)

1968: "Written Composition Outside the English Class" *Journal of English Teaching Techniques* (Emmerich)

By 1975, published accounts of an official university program actually moving writing outside the English department began appearing, with "Teaching Writing Extra-territorially: Carleton College" in the *ADE Bulletin* being the first (Carleton College, 1975).

According to Fulwiler and Young writing in 1982, however, the dissemination of program information was at that time problematic:

> To date few mechanisms have been available for disseminating information about WAC programs in a systematic and comprehensive manner. At present, information about WAC programs is generally shared in three ways: 1) by reading professional English journals such as *College English, College Composition and Communication, Writing Program Administrator,* and *Association of Departments of English Bulletin;* 2) by attending conferences such as the National Council of Teachers of English and/or the Conference on College Composition and Communication—where individual programs and special-interest sessions are conducted; and 3) by inviting writing consultants to campus to introduce program ideas or conduct workshops. The limitations are obvious: only English teachers read the English journals; only those who can afford it—primarily English teachers—attend the English conferences; and the consultants are few, busy and fairly expensive. (Fulwiler and Young, 1982, p. 2)

In recent years, however, a number of forums have grown for the exchange of information. The National Writing Across the Curriculum Conference was first held in 1993 in Charleston, North Carolina. The biannual conference was jointly sponsored by Clemson University, Cornell University, the University of Charleston, and the Citadel. In 1999, the conference was held outside of Charleston for the first time at Cornell University. In 2001, the conference was jointly sponsored by Indiana University, the University of Notre Dame, and Purdue University. In 2002, the conference officially became an annual event with its sixth meeting held at Rice University.

In 1994, the *Journal of Language and Learning Across the Disciplines* was launched as a print journal to "provide a forum for debates concerning interdisciplinarity, situated discourse communities, and writing across the curriculum programs" (http://wac.colostate.edu/atd/archives.cfm). Since 1998 it has been distributed online at the Academic.Writing website which has since become the WAC Clearinghouse website (http://wac.colostate.edu/llad). Back issues are also archived at the location. Another online WAC journal, *Academic.Writing,* founded in 2000, was distributed at the same website (http://wac/colostate.edu/aw/). In 2004 the two journals merged to form *Across the Disciplines* (http://wac.colostate.edu/atd/). These journals provide a place to share program designs, assignments, research, writing theory applied to WAC, discussions of disciplinarity and interdisciplinarity, and discussions of writing within specific disciplines.

The WAC Clearinghouse offers "national support for communication across the curriculum" (http://wac.colostate.edu/). The online clearinghouse offers links to a variety of resources and documents related to WAC, including program descriptions, landmark texts on WAC theory and practice, conferences, research and dissertations related to WAC, and numerous lists of links to additional online information. The WAC Clearinghouse also publishes online new reference, resource, and research books. The journal *Writing Across the Curriculum* is also accessible online through the WAC Clearinghouse. The journal, which began as a regional publication out of Plymouth State College in New Hampshire, has been national in scope since 2000.

The National Network of Writing Across the Curriculum Programs (Elementary-University) facilitates informal support among programs and teachers, including the exchange of ideas and practices. The Network meets at the annual Convention of College Composition and Communication and provides numerous resources at its website (http://wac.gmu.edu/national/network.html).

In many WAC programs, the writing center serves as the nerve center of the program, disseminating information to the university community and providing writing support and services to both faculty and students across disciplines. Consequently, articles on WAC occur frequently in the *Writing Lab Newsletter* and *Writing Center Journal.*

Within university settings, an institution-wide newsletter on the local WAC program is quite common. These newsletters contain personal experience essays from faculty; tips on everything from the creation of assignments to assessment strategies; news about the program's development and implementation; and non-technical articles on composition theories and practices. The publications are as varied as the programs themselves—slick and professional, chatty and informal, top-down or bottom-up, frequent and regular, infrequent and spotty.

3

Programs in Writing Across the Curriculum

Earliest Programs

As far as has been documented, the earliest Writing Across the Curriculum faculty seminar was led by Barbara Walvoord in 1969–70 at Central College (a four-year liberal arts college in Pella, Iowa). As part of the concern for student writing in all majors, a writing proficiency requirement for undergraduate majors was established at the college. Another early program to explore the promise of Writing Across the Curriculum was at Carleton College in Minnesota, also a private four-year liberal arts college. In the early 1970s, Carleton started a cross-curricular program that encouraged faculty to use writing in their courses and eventually ran conferences to train faculty in writing pedagogy and assessment strategies. These early programs were eventually joined by more ambitious programs, funded by outside sources, at Beaver College (also a private four-year school) in Pennsylvania and Michigan Technological University (the first PhD granting and the first public institution to institute a WAC program). In these various programs we see the emergence of key structures that would be used to implement WAC programs: faculty seminars and workshops, writing intensive course requirements, linked courses, the freshman seminar, and peer tutoring. We also see the strong relationship with the National Writing Project that was emerging at the same time, and which was to be a frequent resource and partner with WAC.

The Britton et al (1975) study and the Bullock report (1975) from the UK (see previous chapter) were the subject of a National Endowment for the Humanities summer seminar in 1975—a seminar attended by Michigan Tech faculty member, Toby Fulwiler. Fulwiler returned with new ideas and possibilities for writing in the university and, in collaboration with colleague Art Young, developed a program of faculty workshops, implemented in 1977, that explored ways to use writing in university courses across the departments by integrating writing into existing curricula. The emphasis was "writing to learn" (see Chapter 4) by using journals and ungraded writing assignments to encourage students to explore and develop their thoughts on paper. The program is outlined in Fulwiler and Young's book, *Language Connections: Writing and Reading Across the Curriculum* (1982) (available online at http://wac.colostate.edu/books/language_connections), and the use of journals in university course work is explored in Fulwiler's book, *The Journal Book* (1987a). See also Young and Fulwiler (1986).

At roughly the same time that Toby Fulwiler was encouraging Michigan Tech faculty to integrate writing into their courses, Elaine Maimon was called upon by the dean of Beaver College to do something about the writing crisis. Maimon's program also involved faculty workshops. Her approach, however, focused on "writing as a form of social behavior in the academic community" (McLeod, 1988, p. 4). In her emphasis on the need for students to enter the discourse communities housed in the various college departments, Maimon promoted group work, collaborative projects, and writing intensive courses within the various majors (Maimon, 1982; McLeod & Maimon, 2000). Her program is outlined in her 1981 book, *Writing in the Arts and Sciences*. The approach adopted here is related to what would emerge as the rhetoric of inquiry movement (see Chapter 6).

Writing intensive courses also became the heart of the WAC program at the University of Michigan, where these courses were overseen by an interdisciplinary English Composition Board. The Board organized seminars for faculty development, oversaw syllabi for writing intensive courses, trained teaching assistants, and administered a writing lab. Another solution to increasing emphasis on writing in large courses, the linked course, was pioneered at the University of Washington. In this model small sections of writing courses were linked to large general education lecture courses. Students registered for the lecture course, then had the option to fulfill their writing requirements in the linked writing class, whose assignments would be built around the material and assignments of the lecture course (Russell, 1991, p. 288).

The peer tutoring labs first developed at Brooklyn College (Bruffee, 1978) and California State Dominguez Hills (Sutton, 1978) in 1972. Undergraduate tutors were competitively selected and trained to work with other undergraduates either in a lab or in conjunction with a course. The tutors not only provided support for the writing of the tutees, but together increased their mutual engagement with academic material and the process of writing, creating a more scholarly undergraduate culture.

Cornell University had already begun to reform its freshman writing program as early as 1966 by replacing some sections of the traditional course taught in the English department by seminars taught by professors in nine different disciplines. By the mid-1970s the seminars had grown to largely replace the traditional composition course, and a few years later the freshman seminars became placed within an independently funded unit, which has since become the Knight Institute for Writing in the Disciplines (http://www.arts.cornell.edu/knight_institute/index.html). The Knight Institute now offers a full range of courses in writing in the disciplines at all levels.

The Bay Area Writing Project formed in 1973 as a collaboration between public schools and university writing teachers, and rapidly proved such a successful model for the teaching of writing that within a couple of years it had grown into the National Writing Project, which now has projects in all fifty states. The project formed communities of writing teachers through intensive workshops and continuing activities. Within the workshops teachers were provided experiences to help them perceive themselves as writers and to develop their self-conscious skill as writers. By developing their own writing confidence and competence through interaction with peers, they would then be better prepared to return to their classrooms and establish positive writing environments where all students would write and see themselves as writers. As WAC programs were developing they frequently looked to the Writing Project model of faculty development to design WAC seminars and engage faculty in all disciplines as writers. The idea was, as with the writing projects, that instructors who came to understand themselves as writers and who developed their ability to reflect on writing in their disciplines would be in a better position to expand writing expectations, instruction, and support in their own disciplinary classrooms. They would also become more sympathetic and responsive to students' struggles with writing. Further, some writing projects invited faculty from all disciplines to participate in their seminars, and they became vehicles for introducing WAC to primary and secondary teachers in all subject areas. Such two-way alliances between WAC and local writing projects, for example, developed at George Mason University (which was to become a major force in creating the National Network of WAC Programs) and at the University of North Carolina (which was to run the influential Wildacres Retreats on WAC from 1983–1998).

Writing Across the Curriculum: A Guide to Developing Programs (1992), edited by Susan McLeod and Margot Soven, compares programs in the 1990s with these early programs (available online at http://wac.colostate.edu/books/mcleod_soven/). The early programs, according to McLeod, were funded by external sources and utilized the expertise of outside consultants for their creation. By the 1990s, the majority of WAC programs were reliant upon internal funding in the colleges and universities that housed them. Additionally, the early programs were generally championed by faculty members—in most cases, junior faculty with little administrative clout. The 1990s saw high-ranking college and university administrators enthusiastically promoting WAC programs and prodding sometimes reluctant faculty to bring more writing into courses and general education requirements. In both cases, power moved from a bottom-up movement requiring a certain amount of salesmanship to a top-down institutional mandate.

Many of the WAC-related journal articles published since 1975 have been reports of specific programs designed and implemented at specific institutions (see especially the online journal archives of the *Journal of Language and Learning Across the Disciplines*). Writing program administrators (WPAs) have also conducted research studies on their own programs and those studies are published in journals from time to time, covering topics ranging from faculty motivation to student outcomes (see the journal, *Writing Program Administration*). Toby Fulwiler and Art Young's 1990 book, *Programs That Work: Models and Methods for Writing Across the Curriculum,* provides comprehensive descriptions of fourteen WAC programs, each written by the program administrators from campuses ranging from the two-year college to the PhD granting research university. For further accounts of early

WAC programs, see the new collection, *Creating A Community: The Beginnings of the WAC Movement,* edited by Margot Soven and Susan McLeod (in press).

Administrative & Institutional Support and Interest (1970–1985)[1]

Institutional and administrative interest for writing across the curriculum and writing in the disciplines in the earlier stages of the movement developed largely in response to continued concerns about a perceived literacy crisis among American students. This sense of crisis was in part a response to the expansion of university access fostered by Open Admissions Policies, pioneered at the City University of New York, which guaranteed admissions to any high school graduate. Modified versions of this policy were adopted at a number of public universities in other cities. These policies, which brought new students into the university, made visible the limitations of K-12 education in fostering writing among all students. The challenge of providing all students with the literacy skills necessary for success in a world requiring college education become one of the chief motives for the development of Composition as a professional field.

The first signs of the longstanding struggle among college English professors to teach literacy basics like reading and writing instead of what most preferred—literature—became visible. "The pressure from students who need remedial or basic instruction in writing and from those who are demanding more practical courses in English are forcing some English departments to re-examine their basic approach to the study of English," writes *Chronicle of Higher Education* reporter Malcolm G. Scully in 1974. While for some time high school English teachers had been criticized for allowing literacy standards to slip, col-

---

[1] The institutional support and interest discussed here is measured mainly through articles in American higher education journals. In other words, a review of the major journals that report on the state of higher education was done and not a review of specific universities, departments, or faculty. The support and interest discussed here is gleaned from the opinions of higher education in general as expressed in several of the field's larger and more respected journals.

lege open admissions policies offered college English departments the opportunity to "fix" matters. English departments were not the only ones needing to reconsider their curriculum and pedagogy. "The lack of writing skills [affected] the work of other departments besides English," reports the *Chronicle* (Scully, 1974). A report on undergraduate education in political science for the Carnegie Foundation for the Advancement of Teaching, for example, reported that many students were not strong enough readers and writers to advance in the discipline at an appropriate pace.

The literacy crisis was such a matter of public concern that *Newsweek* declared a state of emergency in American education in a cover story in 1975, posing the problem "Why Johnny Can't Write." *The Chronicle of Higher Education* used extreme headlines such as "Crisis in English Writing" (Scully, 1974) and "Stamping Out Illiteracy" (Berman, 1978) followed by detailed discussions and ample statistics about the declining verbal and written skills of college students. Although few explicit references to writing across the curriculum were made, many of the suggestions aimed at solving the literacy "crisis" involved implementing WAC fundamentals. A research associate at Syracuse University Research Corporation responds with a letter to the editor about the "Crisis" article and questions why "the lion's share of the burden of developing literacy skills is being placed on English departments? Writing is vital to most subjects" (Huff, 1974). She concludes her article with an emphatic assertion that students' exposure to literature should not be limited by the need to develop important writing skills. A letter to the editor by Ronald Reagan's future head of the National Endowment for the Humanities responding to the "Stamp Out Illiteracy" article draws an elaborate analogy between illiteracy and a plague. Joseph C. Voekler, Department of English at Franklin & Marshall College, extends the "disease" metaphor when he comments: "The 'concrete' solution, then, is simple. Infect the students by exposure. Teach the entire faculty—the popular and powerful first, the others later—to know good writing when they see it, to practice it, and to criticize bad writing in an effective way. They have got to stop expecting someone else to do it for them" (Voekler, 1978). Later he speaks directly to the WAC cause by remarking, "It will take expensive faculty workshops on rhetoric in the summers, a writing component in every course the college offers, and the effective persuasion of moss-backed faculty members [to get rid of the disease]"(Voekler, 1978).

Faculty development, a central element of writing across the curriculum theories, gained swift momentum in the 1970s. Also known as "instructional development" or "staff development," it became an extremely popular practice in American higher education. Perhaps one of the biggest reasons for its popularity was that it challenged the long-held belief that college professors' primary goal was research and not teaching. In 1975, Bert Biles, director of a new national center on faculty development at Kansas State University, estimated there were between 400 and 500 such programs on American campuses (Semas, 1975). The programs were characterized by conferences, handbooks, newsletters, and the central belief that teaching did matter as much if not more than research. Jerry G. Gaff, a researcher who conducted a study of these programs for the Exxon Education Foundation, speculates that the "publish or perish [philosophy] will soon be regarded as a quaint piece of academic nostalgia" (1975). Possible reasons for the area's explosive growth included a narrow job market and poor mobility for faculty members; pressures from students, statewide and institutional governing boards, legislatures and governors; and reduced research funding turning more professors' interests towards teaching (Semas, 1975). Although the majority of these faculty-development programs are not foregrounded in WAC, they reflected and informed writing across the curriculum theories, as well as provided an additional motivation for administrators to support WAC programs.

Writing Across the Curriculum in K-12 Education

Although Writing Across the Curriculum developed most visibly in the United States as a higher education initiative, it also resonated with K-12 educators committed to Deweyian models of progressive education. The following anecdote from 1984 indicates how closely WAC was linked to authentic, participatory learning:

> Rich Gottfried, who teaches earth science and chemistry at Chantilly (Va.) High School, was asked how much "extra time" he spent having students write essay tests, rather than fill in the blanks, and helping them develop group projects, rather than just lecturing. "Extra time?" he replied, puzzled. "It's not extra. That's how I teach, and that's how they learn.

> Of what use are facts about rocks and elements if stu-
> dents don't learn to think about those facts the way
> scientists do?" (Thaiss & Suhor, 1982)

Because schools have more resistant and hard-pressed administrative arrangements (see Siskin, 1995), WAC was taken up mostly as a means of improving instruction in individual classrooms rather than as a major school-wide initiative. As a result the major publications of the K-12 WAC movement largely presented easily implemented classroom suggestions rather than describe institutional programmatic development.

Thaiss and Suhor's 1984 volume aimed to "translate the most vital research in writing and oral communication into useful suggestions for classroom practice" (p. ix). It remains a remarkably useful and practical book. Nine essays provide a balance of theory and practice for any teacher (or parent) who wants to understand how writing and speaking across the curriculum can enhance learning. The book is useful for any K-12 practitioner who seeks to understand the theory behind writing to learn and learning to write, as well as some practical classroom implementation strategies.

In *Language Across the Curriculum in the Elementary Grades* (1986), Christopher Thaiss defines language across the curriculum as "something that happens continuously in classrooms and in homes and on playgrounds, whether we wish it to or not" and suggests that much learning can't happen without it (p. 2). Since a child learns about the world through words and symbols, it stands to reason that anything a child is interested in talking or writing about is an opportunity for learning. Thaiss explains that language across the curriculum requires a refocusing of curricula away from content and toward envisioning writing, games playing, and class discussion as opportunities for learning.

Thaiss summarizes the seminal research in this field and introduces the reader to five different elementary classrooms where excellent teachers allow language across the curriculum to work with children of varying learning abilities and disabilities. This book is an excellent reference for any elementary teacher who wants to explore language across the curriculum methods.

Tchudi and Huerta's *Teaching Writing in the Content Areas: Middle School/Junior High* (1983) directs the reader's attention to the why and how of writing in the content areas for middle and junior high students. This small and practical handbook is divided into three parts: Part I—a primer for the novice or experienced writing teacher, Part II—specific examples of writing in the content areas with model units and lessons, and Part III—a source for teachers who want to move on to developing specific materials for their own classrooms. The theme of this publication is "keep content at the center of the writing process" (p. 3). Unlike writing to demonstrate a mastery of the content, the authors believe that writing well follows from creating situations where students want to write, "using their subject-matter knowledge in the process" (p. 3). Recommendations for prewriting and revision activities, as well as guidelines for how to evaluate student writing, are included along with several lesson designs, worksheets, and topic ideas for writing projects in science, math, art/music, social science, history, social studies, civics, career/vocational education, and others that are still practical twenty years after the original publication. Similarly, *Teaching Writing in the Content Areas: Senior High School* by Tchudi and Yates (1983) provides specific model units for high school classrooms.

Part II. Approaches to Theory And Research

4

Research on WAC Teaching and Learning

The programmatic and pedagogical developments in Writing Across the Curriculum are closely associated with three different approaches to theory and research. The first (examined in this chapter) looks closely at classroom practices and student learning to write within disciplines. This research develops detailed ethnographic investigations of students' experiences in writing in various disciplines as well as studies of writing practices in classrooms. This approach has been more closely tied to a concern for the demands of academic writing within university classrooms but includes some studies of K-12 schooling and schools as sites of disciplinary learning. A related research agenda examines reading-writing relationships, addressing the fact that much academic writing is based on materials that students read and then use as a resource or discuss critically. The second, writing to learn (see Chapter 5), grows out of a concern for student-centered engagement with disciplinary materials and thought to be achieved through writing. This approach to writing across the curriculum has been tied to a more general concern for writing to learn in all forms of writing. The final approach, the rhetoric of inquiry (see Chapter 6), grows out of various disciplines' reflections on their own practices and the recognition that forms of writing in a discipline are closely tied to practices of investigation and thought. These approaches are not necessarily opposed and often worked in tandem. But they do show distinct lines of development.

Writing Across the Curriculum has been primarily a programmatic and pedagogical movement, aimed at changing practices in the classroom, increasing the amount of and attention to writing in all classes, improving the assignments, and changing the awareness of teachers in all fields to the role of writing in learning. However research was needed to identify the writing-related practices of students in a variety of classrooms, to determine the way students understood and undertook writing in their subject courses, and to understand how students' writing developed over a series of writing experiences in different courses. Research was also needed to understand how subject-matter teachers assigned and supported writing in their classes, and with what effects. Finally specific interventions carried out in the name of Writing Across the Curriculum needed to be evaluated in their effects on both students and teachers. The following reviews some of the high points of this research literature, but also see Russell's (1994, 2001) two excellent reviews of this material.

Writing Across the Curriculum in K-12 Schooling

The initial and founding study of the WAC movement, Britton, et al's *Development of Writing Abilities,* researched what existing writing practices were occurring in disciplinary classrooms (see Chapter 2). More recent research into writing across the curriculum in K-12 classrooms, however, is for the most part tied to educational interventions. These studies ranging across the K-12 spectrum have found that writing has supported subject area learning and thinking, in line with the Writing to Learn theoretical orientation (see Chapter 5). While the sophistication of the subject matter engagement changes over the course grades the use of writing to increase understanding, involvement, subject learning, and disciplinary thought remains consistent.

Primary School

Wollman-Bonilla (1998) introduced scientific writing into a first grade classroom in the form of Family Message Journals, wherein students a variety of texts to be read and responded to by their families, including poems and fiction as well as informational texts about what they learned and did in school. Writing the science parts of the journal would typically follow a hands-on science activity in the class; the writing prompt would simply be to write to your family what the class had just done. While the teachers offered no formal instruction on how science should be written, they did model the kinds of phrasing the students might use. In this context it was found that first-graders were able to write original texts about science that incorporated a number of the genre features of science reports, explanations, and experimental recounts and procedures, including appropriate text structure, lexical choices and grammatical forms.

Winograd (1993) studied eight fifth graders as "they composed original mathematics story problems." Usually math problems are authored by adults for students to solve; students seldom have an opportunity to develop problems of their own. Winograd suggests that his study can provide "a theoretical and practical point of departure for problem-writing approach to school mathematics" (Winograd, 1993, p. 372). He observes that students developed three strategies to compose problems: they asked questions to identify the general topic; they created a final question to which they addressed their texts; they worked to increase the difficulty of their problems. This study suggests that "students may be able to collaborate effectively with teachers in writing mathematics curriculum" (Winograd, 1993, p. 369).

Johnson, Jones, Thornton, Langrall, and Rous (1998) also studied fifth graders writing in the mathematics classroom. The students did journal writing before and after each probability task where they described their thinking and reasoning about probability. At the completion of the program five of the eight target students made gains in both probability and writing. Although the team was not surprised to find that students used both writing and mathematical symbols as they wrote about probability (see Bruner, 1964; Biggs & Collis, 1991), they had not expected the solutions of these fifth graders to rely so heavily on these two types of representation. They attribute these outcomes to the use of a cognitive apprenticeship model by the teacher who encouraged the students to write up their mathematical solutions in the same way a mathematician at work would.

High School

Kathleen McCarthy Young and Gaea Leinhardt (1998) observed five high school students in an AP History classroom. The teacher used primary and secondary sources instead of an authoritative but "authorless textbook" in her effort to introduce these students to a more sophisticated way of knowing history—not as a list of facts but rather as constructed and interpreted from various artifacts and documents.

The students engaged in four major Document-Based Question writing tasks. The authors analyzed both the tasks and the texts produced by the five students to assess their progress in mastering not only the content but also the rhetorical strategies of the discipline

Young and Leinhardt argue that academic literacy requires both knowledge in the specific domain and understanding of the rhetorical practices of that domain. The primary purpose of this study was to "explore what was involved in writing from primary documents and in learning to do so, rather than to examine empirically the question of whether students learned more history by writing from documents" (Young & Leinhardt, 1998, p. 27). Young and Leinhardt view discipline-based reading, writing, and reasoning as situated processes and forms. These specialized ways of knowing are not always easily accessible to those who need to learn them and recognize that students are brought into the ways of the discipline through "enculturation, apprenticeship, and scaffolded participation" (p. 27).

The authors recognized that the teaching practices of the subject teacher that engaged the students in the discipline of history do "support the development of complex writing skills even when these writing skills are not the object of explicit instruction" (Young & Leinhardt, 1998, p. 59). But they argue that because of minimal in-class writing opportunities, the students need to negotiate written arguments and explanations without benefit of models or coaching. They recommend that excellent instruction practices like these coupled with writing instruction, in-class writing, peer review, opportunities for revision and teacher feedback, would further support the development of academic literacy.

Olga Dysthe's (1996) qualitative research study of three high school classrooms examines how the interaction of talking and writing affects learning. The study presents a writing centered dialogic model of teaching strategies informed by the theoretical work of Bakhtin (1986), Vygotsky (1986), and Nystrand (1990). Inspired by the resistance of classroom teachers to pedagogical reform movements (demonstrated by the research which indicates that in the classroom, teachers talk 75% of the time, students 25%) Dysthe observed two American classrooms (American History and AP European History) and one Norwegian (social science). The article follows Nystrand and Gamoran's (1991) distinction between common classroom interaction (what is sometimes called IRE—initiation, response, evaluation) and the interactive, dialogic pattern of interaction. This dialogic inter-action includes "authentic questions," (where the teacher asks open-ended questions); "uptake,"(student response is incorporated in her subsequent questions); and "high-level evaluation," (the teacher elabo-rates on the student response and builds on it in following interac-tions). Teachers' ideologies and practices are discussed and the lessons presented and evaluated within the framework of the dialogic model. Dysthe provides examples of how interrelating writing and talk pro-motes student participation and a greater diversity of student voic-es. Because it values students as thinkers and their texts as legitimate "thinking devices," students gain academic self-confidence.

Talk and Writing in Secondary Science

Rivard & Straw (2000) investigate further the roles of talk and writ-ing for science learning for a group of Francophone Canadian eighth graders, instructed in English. This study uses a mix of qualitative and quantitative methods in a quasi-experimental design, studying stu-dents under four conditions. Following lessons on ecology, groups of students engaged in discussion-only activities, writing-only activities, combined discussion and writing activities, or a control group with no supplementary activities. The supplementary activities involved solv-ing ecological problems that relied on concepts presented in the les-sons. Students' knowledge was assessed immediately after the learning activities and again after six weeks. Overall, the authors found that a combination of talk and writing provided the greatest improvement—with talk serving to share and clarify knowledge, and writing serving to refine and consolidate knowledge with prior knowledge. Writing further seems to serve to aid retention of co-constructed knowledge. Interestingly there were strong indications that the value of talk and writing may vary with student ability. Those students most skilled in the subject area benefited most of individual writing without discus-sion, while those least skilled benefited most from discussion. This finding is consistent with the overall view that discussion and writing serve different functions, with skilled students able to gather informa-tion on their own and benefiting from refinement and consolidation, and less killed students needing support in gathering and understand-ing the information.

Keys (1999) reviews the literature that suggests the need for more attention to writing in the science classrooms for purposes of science learning. In a follow-up study Keys (2000) investigates more deeply into the kinds of thinking students do in the course of writing experimental reports. She used think-aloud methods to examine the thought processes of sixteen eighth grade science students writing up a laboratory activity on the topic of erosion. While five of the sixteen students engaged in no reflective thought and simply recording information, the remainder engaged in a variety of forms of thinking. Two focused on rhetorical planning of organization and sequence, and the remaining nine engaged in forms of scientific problem solving. These problems included generating hypotheses and developing general claims, identifying evidence and finding patterns in the data. They found they needed to solve these problems in order to determine what they should be writing.

Prain and Hand (1999), in an ethnographic study of writing in secondary science instruction in Australia, similarly found that writing served different thinking and learning functions for different students on different occasions. Using semi-structured interviews along with observation and text collection, found that writing provided students opportunities to "reorder, synthesize, elaborate, and reprocess concepts and ideas central to each topic, to hypothesize, interpret and persuade" (p. 151). Students perceived that with writing their engagement was more active and involved higher order cognition. Because of the variety of functions served by writing, the authors suggest diversification in writing types assigned.

To foster more reflective thinking and enhanced student learning from laboratory activities, Keys, Hand, Prain, and Collins (1999) have developed a Science Writing Heuristic. This heuristic has a teacher component and a student component. The teacher component provides an eight-step structure for teacher-designed activities that provides for exploratory preliminary activities using concept mapping, informal writing, and brainstorming. It also provides for a multi-stepped series of writings following the laboratory activity help students determine the meanings of the experiment, interpret the data, and relate the results to the textbooks or other literature. The student component gets students to reflect on their questions, actions, observations, claims, evidence, reading, and what they have learned. The Science Writing Heuristic was found effective in advancing student knowledge and thought over an eight week learning sequence in two eighth grade classes. Follow-up studies have found the Science Writing Heuristic effective in both secondary (Hand, Wallace, & Yang in press; Hand, Prain, & Wallace 2002; Hand & Prain, 2002) and higher education science courses (Rudd, Greenbowe, Hand, & Legg, 2001; Rudd, Greenbowe, & Hand, 2001).

Subject Organization of Secondary Schools as an Obstacle to WAC

According to Siskin and Little's *The Subjects in Question: Departmental Organization and the High School* subject organization of high schools has proven to be remarkably enduring and resistant to interdisciplinary cooperations such as Writing Across the Curriculum. This volume comes out of a five-year study by the Center for Research on the Context of Secondary School Teaching (CRC). While not directly addressing Writing Across the Curriculum, this volume provides valuable insight into disciplinary organization of high schools which any secondary WAC program must address. Siskin's opening chapter on Subject Division, in particular, finds that the departmentally divided social words of secondary educators strongly limits teacher interaction, Length of teacher's employment at one school and school size correlate with departmental orientation. Not only time and space arrangements reinforce subject divisions but also the almost magnetic pull of subjects on teachers who wanted to discuss the specifics of their work. The volume then examines this dilemma from the perspectives of organizational theory, professional identity and response to institutionally imposed reforms, and ideology and politics. The functional strengths of departmental culture are also explored. Case studies are drawn from English, social studies, and other departments. Proposals and implemented projects to foster collaborative and interdisciplinary cultures among secondary teachers are also examined.

Writing Across the Curriculum in Higher Education

While some studies of writing across the curriculum in higher education have examined the impact of specific interventions in WAC environments, the larger number of studies have focused on the experiences and development of students involving writing in their disciplinary courses and of teachers as they have come to employ writing in their courses. This difference in focus perhaps reflects the different culture of higher education, the more developed identities and skills of students, and the greater academic freedom of professors to set goals for, design, evaluate and change their instruction. Consonant with the differences in research focus, higher intervention studies have tended to be more ethnographic, often over extended time, rather than quantitative studies of changed outcomes after intervention.

MacDonald and Cooper's (1992) study of writing to learn in a Chinese Literature course, discussed in the next chapter, indicates that use of journals must be well-matched to the goals and tasks of the major assignments by which the students will be evaluated. Herrington's (1988) study of writing in a literature class again suggests that students will learn what they are asked to do and will adopt the writing elements they are asked for, which are practiced, and which are given support. Students' perceptions of the assignment and the tasks they must accomplish are shaped by the assignments, the roles instructors project, the interchange of the classroom, as well as the interpretive strategies that they are taught and practice in class discussion. In this case the teacher of literature through the student-choice built into the assignment and the exploratory atmosphere of class discussion was able to lead students into independent inquiry, which was her pedagogic goal. Where the class fell short was in providing sufficient tools to carry that inquiry forward, and the prior familiarity of the students with these tools accounted for the differential success on the papers.

The implicit messages and goals of a course may be so effective in defining the writing asked for that motivated students will adopt the valued forms of writing even without instruction—taking their cues from the modeling provided by the professor, the readings, and the general cultural understanding of the domain. This at least is the conclusion drawn from Freedman, Adam, and Smart's 1994 study "Wearing Suits to Class." They found students in an undergraduate financial analysis course designed to simulate workplace experiences adopted outward signs of workplace behavior and carried out analytical tasks typical of the workplace on case materials. Moreover the form and format of their written reports, oral presentations, and documents accompanying the presentation bore a resemblance to workplace presentations. All this was accomplished without specific writing guidance by the instructor, but with substantial modeling of tasks and language in classroom lectures and activities. Freedman, Adam, and Smart further report that "a stance and an ideology were realized through the writing that—like their suits—were more like the stances, values, and ways of constructing, construing, and persuading common to the work world to which these students aspired" (1994, p. 220). The students seemed keen to adopt the professional manner and substance offered by the professor and were motivated to socialize themselves into a professional world they wanted to be part of. This motivated anticipatory socialization was a powerful force for students to align with the models of communication presented in class.

Student Goals and Course Goals

Research on other writing in other classrooms, however, finds that such congruent alignment often does not exist. The lack of alignment to the professional world offered by the course then creates distance between students and their writing assignments, which they do not see as meaningful. The mismatch of the alignment and motivation of students with the goals of the courses, is an underlying problem that emerges from a number of ethnographic studies of undergraduate writing within disciplinary classes. The initial and landmark study of student writing in a variety of courses is Lucille McCarthy's (1987) "Stranger in Strange Lands." This study uses observation, interview, compose-aloud, and text analysis to follow a single student through writing in three courses over his first two years in college: composition, introduction to poetry and cell biology. The writing experience in each of these courses was distinctive, requiring different kinds of writing in different learning contexts, although each of the teachers had similar goals of developing students academic thinking and writing in disciplinary appropriate ways. The difference was that each represented a different disciplinary perspective. The student's response to the differences of disciplinary perspective was to see little continuity in the writing across the three classes and he had very different success in each. In two of the cases he saw four personal, professional, and institutional functions for the writing, different for each course, but congruent with each instructor's goals. But in the third course he saw the only purpose was institutional: to demonstrate his academic competence. Consequently he found little personal meaning from the assignments in this third course He summed up his experience of writing in cynical terms: "First you have to figure out what your teachers want. And then you have to give to them if you're gonna' get the grade. [. . .] And that's not always easy." (McCarthy, 1987, p. 362)

For teachers of writing it is also not easy to determine what disciplinary faculty want. That is the conclusion drawn by Faigley and Hansen's (1985) study of writing in two social science classes. They found that while English teachers responded to the form, disciplinary instructors were more concerned with familiarity with disciplinary knowledge and modes of reasoning, and thus looked to the conceptual depth and evidence of the argument, as viewed through disciplinary lenses. Schwegler and Shamoon (1991) looked further into the criteria eight sociologists used in grading student papers and found the professors had a highly developed model of what kind of work counted as good sociology. This model rested on analogies with existing studies, such that in grading the professor would quickly identify the student as trying to accomplish a particular kind of study and would measure the paper against the kind of evidence and analysis appropriate to that kind of work. The professors were stricter in evaluating the design, evidence and analysis of the study than they were in evaluating the introduction and review of literature. They could identify the point of the study even if the students were not able to articulate well what they aware doing or did not have good command of the literature. This study suggests how particular and discipline bound are disciplinary evaluations of student work. (See Chapter 9 for further discussion of evaluation of student writing within WAC courses).

But what disciplinary faculty may want to teach and evaluate students upon are not always what students want to get from a course or excited by Herrington's 1985 study of writing in two chemical engineering courses. She found first that the instructors of the two courses in the same discipline had different goals, assignments, purposes for assigning writing, roles for student to adopt in their writing, and criteria for evaluating work. Second, she found that students perceptions of what was required differed from the instructors', in part because of the conflicting expectations presented by the two instructors and what was necessary to fulfill the expectations. As a result there were distinctive differences in the papers of the two courses, and uneven student success. Further because of the structure of one of the courses, the students could not form a consistent communication with a single instructor, could not develop a common set of roles and stances, and found the assignments frustrating and not engaging. In the other course where students could develop a stability of expectations, there was greater satisfaction and engagement.

Similar problems of student lack of engagement appeared in Greene's 1993 study of upper division history students. Students felt the assignment did not ask or invite them to go beyond displaying familiarity with the set readings, so they neither drew on background knowledge nor engaged in analysis. Even when given a problem-based assignment, students tended only to report information from resources rather than using information and resources to construct an argument. They viewed the assignments as school exercises rather than occasions for professional inquiry. Lack of student alignment to instructor set goals and tasks are also examined in Marsella, Hilgers, and McClaren (1992), Nelson (1990), and Herrington (1981).

Dias, Freedman, Medway, and Pare's (1999) comparative study of academic and workplace writing in four areas (public administration, business, social work, and architecture) found that the instructional and evaluation aspects of writing within college courses consistently shaped how students responded to writing assignments, even when courses were designed as workplace simulations. The teacher as evaluative always remained the most important audience. Thus university writing could only call on a limited part of students' anticipation of professional identities and attraction to the work and rewards the profession would offer.

Similar alienation from the tasks of academic writing was encountered in Chiseri-Strater's longitudinal study of two undergraduate students reported in the 1991 book, *Academic Literacies*. Both students were academically capable but did not find much meaning in most of their assignments. One near the end of her undergraduate career manages to finally locate a personal engagement with a paper in art history, helping explore her own aesthetic commitments through the examination of a painter she admires. The other student spends much effort in clever displays of skill, but develops an increasingly cynical, distant and power-based view about knowledge and reason. This corresponds to his migration to political science. But underneath the struggles and frustration with the academic languages of these two students is a struggle to come to discover what it is they know, what it is they are committed to, and how those perceptions and commitments can be enacted in professional and academic ways.

It is these personal journeys of students through the years of their undergraduate education that becomes the theme of *Persons in Process,* by Anne Herrington and Marcia Curtis (2000). This study follows four students through the undergraduate years, each working through personal issues of identity, career and commitment. The papers they write for their various courses all are part of that personal journey, and get their meaning and motive from it. Nam, a Vietnamese immigrant, works to be able to explain himself and his beliefs to others in his new language. This means a commitment to learning the conventions, but also to discovering the genre of essay as a site for expressing himself. Not only does he work through issues of identity, emotion, and ethnicity, he starts to articulate his religious beliefs. As he encountered his academic subjects such as psychology and philosophy his wariness abut the secular knowledge they offered and his difficulties with the subtleties of language kept his work sticking close to the facts, formally correct but without substantial engagement. He soon transferred to a seminary, which he found more satisfying. Yet it was his experience of coming to know himself through the essays in the writing class, and recognizing the disengaged experiences in his other course that helped him articulate what it was he wanted and where he needed to go.

Another student, the child of an alcoholic family, entered the university lacking confidence. Her journey through the university was also one of understanding and growing confidence. Her journey led her to an honors thesis in psychology on how the young adult children of alcoholics cope with intimacy. For her the study of psychology provided tools to understand her family and herself, and each essay she wrote, whether in her major or another area, if it helped advance that self-understanding, was engaging. If not, it seemed pro forma. She found a paper for a women's studies course meaningful but not another on globalism, and she did not do nearly as well on it. Each of the four detailed case studies in the volume is nuanced and revealing about the meaning and motivation students find in college writing, and thus what challenges they address in fulfilling the assignments. From the student's perspective, writing is best understood not so much in the terms of the course where the assignment is made (although that forms the occasion and provides the discipline specific tools and resources) but in the terms of their lives. Even each distanced relationship they construct when they let an assignment pass by on the periphery of their attention has a particular flavor and a particular sense in relation to their life paths.

Geisler (1994) similarly found that undergraduate students in philosophy courses approached their papers differently than did graduate students or professors. While the professors and the professionalizing graduate students understood philosophic texts as addressing problems, situated within a long literature and needing an abstract solution that would persuade other philosophers, students viewed philosophic texts more personally and practically. They used their readings and writing assignments to help them address personal ethical issues in their own lives and used their experiences to help them understand what the philosophers were saying.

While students often find meaning, value, and motivated commitment in personal issues, professors typically design courses around goals of developing disciplinary or professional knowledge and skills. In some situations, students seem to have more professionalized identities than others. Jolliffe and Brier (1988), for example, in a pilot study examining the performance of nursing students and political science students on a writing task of abstracting professional articles, found that the more professional experience the students had the better they did these tasks. Further that given the structure of the programs the nursing students had both more experience and professional training, and correspondingly overall did better on the task. Similarly, Haas (1994) found that a biology student over the four years of her undergraduate experience found that the student developed a more sophisticated style of reading as she became familiar with the field. This sophistication would have an affect on the stance she would take in her own writing. She not only gained content knowledge and thus could understand the biology more easily, but she began to read the articles rhetorically. She began to see the scientific authors as agents, arguing for claims within specific historical and intertextual contexts. In reading more as a professional scientist, she identified more as a working member of the profession, and understood her own work to be similarly making situated arguments.

Medway, in studying the writing of architecture students both in and out of class saw writing being part of developing professional commitments and identities. Writing bears a very different relation to the training and professionalization of architects (Medway 2000). While architecture students did much writing, the writing was not the primary student product nor the basis for evaluation. It was the design projects and other graphic artifacts that were the basis of evaluation.

Nor did the writing resemble the writing they would do as professional architects. Rather the writing was part of thinking through and explaining designs, a by-product of the primary work—but nonetheless an important necessity. As the students were committed to their profession and found the writing necessity, and as the writing was never evaluated or even examined by standards extraneous to the task, it was not seen as a problem. Moreover the students grew in articulateness without especial monitoring of their language, but rather as part of their deeper engagement in the profession. The personal sketchbooks they kept (Medway, 2002) strikingly exemplifies the role of writing in forming their architectural identities, styles, and creative imaginations. Although not assigned or part of any course, nor a practice generally followed by professional architects once they completed their training, most of the architectural student in the group studied kept one. In it they kept everything from addresses and personal diary entries to sketches for design projects. They recorded quotations from readings and lectures, principles that struck them as important; they pasted or interleaved photos and prints of art and architecture, business cards, maps; they drew what they saw and were designing and included explanatory notes and captions; they wrote evaluations of things they saw and developed arguments their ideas and proposals. The drawing, writing and collecting was all done aesthetically and together developed a personal style. In providing a personal place for the students to draw, imagine, plan, evaluate professionally, these sketchbooks represent the fusion of personal and professional, where students display emergent professional selves to themselves.

Studies of WAC Instructors and Instruction

While most studies of WAC in higher education have focused on students and student writing, a number of studies have looked at the way teachers across the disciplines use writing in their classes and have modified their instruction under the influence of WAC programs.

WAC seminars and other faculty supports have been shown in several studies to have influenced faculty participants in adopting WAC beliefs and use WAC strategies in their courses (Smithson & Sorrentino, 1987; Kalmbach & Gorman, 1986; Hughes-Weiner & Jensen-Cekalla, 1991). More detailed case studies reveal something of the personal transformation that instructors undergo as they participate in WAC workshops and programs (Sipple, 1987; Kipling & Murphy, 1992), although accounts also note faculty resistance (Swilky, 1992) or other failure to fully implement a WAC orientation (Johnstone, Johnstone, & Balester, 1994).

An in-depth study of 300 writing intensive courses in the natural and applied sciences on one campus found that instructors of these courses adopted a range of stances to the writing, from corrector to journal editor to collaborator (Chinn & Hilgers, 2000). Instructors that adopted more of a collaborative stance assigned a wider range of activities and writing tasks with more varied audiences; provided more explicit guidelines for writing; had students consider professional contexts for writing; and encouraged interaction, collaboration and peer-reviewing among students. Such instructors also tended to be more successful in engaging students in writing and gaining student approval.

Russell and Yanez (2003), however, have found that writing in general education courses, in this instance one in Irish history, suffers a contradiction between the specialist disciplinary activity systems of disciplinary training and the lay orientation of non-majors in general education courses. This contradiction makes it difficult for students to reach beyond fact-based rote writing and leads to student alienation. Skillful and attentive instruction is needed to guide students toward meaningful higher order thinking in the writing without expecting them to take on the disciplinary roles appropriate to committed majors in the discipline.

A nuanced and in-depth study of instructors' experiences in implementing WAC in their classrooms is presented in Walvoord and McCarthy's *Thinking and Writing in College* (1990). This ethnographic account examines writing assignment, support and instruction along with student difficulties and success in university courses in business, history, sexuality, and biology. Through a detailed examination of the courses the researchers identified the distinct professional-in-training roles: in business the decision maker; in history the arguer using historical evidence; in psychology the social scientist or counselor; and in biology the research scientist. They also found distinct differences in the kinds of evaluations the students were expected to make. However, in all courses the researchers were able to identify student difficulties in the same six areas: "gathering sufficient specific information; constructing the audience and the self; stating a position; suing appropriate discipline-based methods [...]; managing complexity; [and] organizing the paper" (Walvoord & McCarthy, 1990, p. 231). From the investigation they derived nine principles for guiding thinking and writing in disciplinary courses.

1. Make the teaching methods fit the writing and thinking processes of the high achieving students.

2. Present procedural knowledge procedurally.

3. Define clear goals for informal, ungraded writing.

4. Guide peer response.

5. Make teacher draft response consistent with the writing process and the reward system.

6. Craft the assignment sheet with care.

7. Give explicit instructions and guidance, especially when designating a peer audience and/or a familiar setting and topic for student writing.

8. Offer early guidance.

9. Use language in the modes you want students to use. (Walvoord & McCarthy, 1990, pp. 238–241)

Walvoord then led another research team to look at the long-term effects on faculty of continuing participation in WAC programs on three different campuses (Walvoord, Hunt, Dowling, & McMahon 1997). They found that the primary effects of participation were to deepen faculty's reflective understanding of their teaching philosophies and choices, rather than to adopt a particular set of beliefs or classroom practices. Faculty came to the seminars already primed with their own issues, goals, and reflective practices. While they adopted some WAC strategies presented, they chose selectively depending on whether it work for them in creating community in the classroom, in furthering student learning, in being feasible within the organizations of their classroom, and in matching their own priorities and teaching style. Over the years their engagement with WAC followed different patterns, ranging from leaving it on the back burner or displacing it for another mode of teaching reform to offering a radical turning point in their teaching and/or other aspects of their career. In the middle were patterns of selective choice and gradual evolution.

The most detailed examination of the effect of WAC on an instructor comes from the long-term collaboration between Stephen Fishman, a philosopher, and Lucille McCarthy, a writing researcher. Over a number of years as McCarthy has observed and done studies of Fishman's introductory courses, they have engaged in a reflective dialogue which has led Fishman to look more deeply into his goals as a teacher of philosophy, what his students were learning, and the nature of the classroom interaction. They document the observations and thinking that develops over the course of this collaboration in a series of articles (Fishman, 1993; Fishman & McCarthy, 1992, 1995, 1996; McCarthy & Fishman, 1991, 1996) and finally two books *John Dewey and the Challenge of Classroom Practice* (Fishman & McCarthy, 1998) and *Unplayed Tapes* (Fishman & McCarthy, 2000). As researcher and teacher look ever more closely at his classroom practices, Fishman finds his assumptions constantly being overturned and ever more doubt about what he believes the students are learning and expressing in their class discussion and their writing. Using Fishman's commitment to Dewey as a starting point and continuing touchstones, Fishman and McCarthy uncover the intricacies of truly establishing a truly student-centered curriculum engaged in serious dialogue about those things that matter to students, so that they will come to see the value of a philosophic and experimental examination of their own lives and will develop the skill to engage in it. .

Studies of Graduate Students

In graduate education students have to address more directly and completely the professional writing of their disciplines, often within a more closely supervised and mentored environment. Blakeslee (1997, 2001) investigates such graduate learning through apprenticeship in physics, where a professor assigns the student real, but calibrated significant tasks in the course of research, provides detailed feedback on drafts, and creates situations that will extend the student's scope. On the other hand, when time or other exigencies press, the professor takes greater control of the texts. Schryer, Lingard, Spafford, and Garwood (2003) offer another example of students learning agency in their profession, in this case medical students in learning how to present cases on rounds. Although this is an oral task, it is as composed and rhetorically designed to be professionally useful as any written report.

While one might think that in graduate situations there would be few problems of professional commitment and alignment with the values of the discipline, several studies have found such difficulties indeed arise as students work examine the how well the values and work of the field match with their own personal commitments and goals, particularly in the earlier years of graduate training (Casanave, 1995). Also students need to find their own interests and questions within the field, which then leads to differential engagement with different assignments as well as exploration of how to develop some conjunction of personal with professional to pursue within assignments (Prior, 1998).

Even when aligned to tasks and discourses grad students not only need to synthesize more materials, frame complex problems, juggle more data, and develop deeper arguments they must also sort through the various judgments and potential influences offered by their professors and peers. And they need to develop a responsibility and confidence in their choices that allows them to make their arguments clearly and forcefully. They need to come to an understanding of what professional authorship means and how they can enact it. Further all this is located within historically evolving disciplines and the students' biographies and emerging careers. Paul Prior investigates these complexities of writing oneself into a discipline and thereby remaking the discipline are investigated in a series of detailed studies brought together in his book *Writing/Disciplinarity* (1998).

Reading/Writing Connection: Specialized Forms of Reading

The teaching and study of academic writing, and particularly writing across the curriculum has led to an understanding about the relationship between reading on writing, based on the concrete uses academic writers make of their reading in their textual productions. In academic and disciplinary writing students and professionals specifically refer to and cite material they have read as well as implicitly rely on other ideas and knowledge gleaned from reading. Thus summary, paraphrase, synthesis, response, critique, and research writing are important reading-based writing skills. Moreover, the exercise of these forms of writing relies on accurate reading and displays the quality of the writer's reading. Further, the need for materials to write about and one's commitment to making a statement can motivate and direct interpretation in reading. (Bazerman 1980, 1981).

Flower, et al. (1990) examine more deeply what happens when students read-to-write. They find that for many students, source texts are not transparent repositories of information which can be extracted and then recreated in the student's own writing. Even when students have little trouble accessing information from a source text, they have several more steps to navigate before they can begin to create a new text. Flower, et al. call this "building a representation of the source text" (p. 125), and argue that students use this representation to create a representation of their own original text. In addition, Flower argues that the mental construction readers make of a text, even when reading for the "simple" task of comprehension, is in itself a significant piece of work that "can do much of the work reading-to-write calls for" (p. 247). (See also Spivey, 1990.)

Risemberg (1996) found there is a relationship between the length of time students spend reading information related to their writing assignments and the quality of the writing produced. Students who engaged more extensively with models of an essay similar to the one they were writing and/or a set of guidelines for writing that kind of essay—an activity he called task-information seeking—produced better writing. In addition, Risemberg found that this factor has a paradoxical relationship with reading ability and other variables. On the one hand, task-information seeking uniquely predicts writing quality when other variables such as reading ability and self-efficacy are included; on the other hand, reading ability and task-information seeking themselves showed no correlation. In fact, task-information seeking correlated with none of the other variable, only outcome. Thus, it was not necessarily the weaker or stronger writers who engaged in this activity, nor was there a relationship between task-information seeking and self-efficacy. Another related finding was that the stage at which a writer seeks task information seems crucial. Those who consulted the informational texts during the note-taking and reading stage were produced better texts than those who did so during the writing stage.

Similarly, Johns and Lenski (1997) found that the organization of student writing is influenced in part by the reading they do in the course of researching. This influence was found to emanate not only from the kinds of reading students in their study did, such as reference books versus trade books, but also the kinds of reading behaviors students engaged in—skimming versus reading—the number of texts consulted, and the pattern of searching, reading, and writing that the students exhibited. The strongest relationship seemed to occur with the pattern of researching and the resulting text. The researchers found three distinct patterns—sequential, spiral, and recursive—and correlating patterns in final texts.

Finally, WAC researchers have noted that students need to learn to engage in specific forms of reading in different subject areas. Haas (1994) observed that over the four years of an undergraduate major a biology student became a more sophisticated interpreter and user of texts in biology as she became involved in the networks of activities, people, and knowledge that were part of the communal enterprise of biology. Geisler (1994) found that not only did philosophers have very particular readings and uses of the philosophic literature in their own writings, but that these differed significantly from the readings and uses displayed by undergraduates. The differences were not simply explainable by the level of sophistication and knowledge, but also had to do with the difference of stance, with students reading philosophy in relation to their personal life issues, while philosophers read texts as presenting positions in an abstracted argument about knowledge.

5

Writing to Learn

Origins of the Writing to Learn Approach

Writing to Learn is based on the observation that students' thought and understanding can grow and clarify through the process of writing. A saying attributed to E.M. Forster, "How can I know what I think until I see what I say" (Auden, 1962) captures the spirit of this approach and is widely cited by its adherents. This observation has been elaborated, researched, and made the heart of a pedagogy that focuses on personal, expressivist, journal, and other forms of exploratory writing.

James Britton and Janet Emig are primarily responsible for turning this observation into a pedagogical approach. In 1966, the Dartmouth Seminar brought together English language scholars from the United States and England and paved the way for a positive reception of the distinctly British model of language instruction put forth by Britton (1970) and Britton, et al. (1975). In contrast to the American emphasis on "disciplinary rigor, standard curricula, and standard 'objective' evaluation," (Russell, 1994, p. 11) Britton, et al. (1975) identified three functional types of writing: transactional, for communicating information; poetic, for creating beautiful objects; and expressive, for exploring and reflecting upon ideas. Important to the writing to learn movement is this last category, expressive writing, which he and his colleagues argued could play a cardinal role in learning at every developmental stage, in part because it resembled what Vygotsky had identified as "inner speech" (p. 39). By foregrounding the personal and psychological utility of writing in learning settings (Britton, et al. 1975), and by emphasizing the powerful ways in which language organizes experience (Britton, 1970), Britton and his colleagues lent substantial credence to the idea that cross-curricular writing programs could enhance student learning.

Meanwhile, the process-over-product movement had begun with the publication of Janet Emig's (1971) landmark work, *The Composing Processes of Twelfth Graders*. By studying the think-aloud protocols of eight 12th-grade writers, Emig persuasively presented writing as a complex, recursive process worthy of being studied and taught in its own right. Equally important to the writing to learn movement was her 1977 landmark article, "Writing as a Mode of Learning," which stands as a sort of charter document for the writing to learn movement. Because writing is neurophysiologically integrative, connective, active, and available for immediate visual review, speculated Emig, it represents a unique form of learning that deserves increased experimental and theoretical attention.

By 1983, a noticeable body of literature had amassed, uniformly celebrating writing as a central learning process (see Humes, 1983, for a review of this research). Applebee (1984, p. 582) has summarized the results of this research corpus as follows:

1. Writing involves a variety of recursively operating subprocesses (e.g., planning, monitoring, drafting, revising, editing) rather than a linear sequence.

2. Writers differ in their uses of the processes.

3. The processes vary depending on the nature of the writing task.

Also following Emig (1971, 1977) were studies that focused on writing in more constrained environments. Notetaking, for example, was seen as a potentially telling research site at the intersection of writing and learning. Di Vesta and Gray (1972), Fisher and Harris (1973), Schultz and di Vesta (1972), Kulhavy, Dyer, and Silver (1975), and Applebee (1984, pp. 585–586) found that notetaking was a more effective study technique than reading or listening alone, although the results depended on the notetaking strategy adopted as well as on whether the notes were available for later review. These studies also suggested that notetaking was a more effective study technique than the traditional study method of underlining. However, because the notetakers spent more time on task than the readers, listeners, and underliners, the question of whether the results were due to some special quality of writing or simply a function of time on task remained unexamined (see Bretzing & Kulhavy, 1979, for a notable exception).

More Recent Developments

In 1984, Newell, lamenting the lack of empirical backing for writing as a mode of learning, examined the effects of notetaking, short-answer responses, and essay writing on three measures of learning: recall, concept application, and gain in passage-specific knowledge. He found that essay writing enabled students to "produce a consistently more abstract set of associations for key concepts than did notetaking or answering study questions," (p. 275) and provided a possible explanation for such a finding based on Emig's notion of the connective nature of writing:

> [A]nswering study questions required planning at a local level rather than at a global level. While answering study questions may require a great deal of planning, the writer can only consider information in isolated segments. Consequently, while a great deal of information is generated, it never gets integrated into a coherent text, and, in turn, into the students' own thinking. Essay writing, on the other hand, requires that the writers, in the course of examining evidence and marshaling ideas, integrate elements of the prose passage into their knowledge of the topic rather than leaving the information in isolated bits. This integration may well explain why students' understanding of concepts from the prose passage was significantly better after writing essays than after answering study questions. (Newell, 1984, p. 282)

Since time spent on task remained uncontrolled (Applebee, 1984, p. 587), however, questions remain, as with the studies on notetaking, whether we can rightful attribute the statistically significant difference between interventions to anything other than the duration of exposure to the subject matter. However, it may also be that the notetaking and writing tasks were useful devices to create sufficiently challenges to hold attention on the subject matter for a longer time.

Five years later, Newell teamed up with Winograd to re-examine Newell's (1984) data with two new constructs—"level of importance" and "quality of gist"—in mind. Besides confirming Newell's (1984) earlier findings, Newell and Winograd (1989) concluded that both short-answer responses and essay writing enabled students to "recall the overall organizing frames of the original passages more often than when they engaged in notetaking" and that the more holistic "recall of gist" was best facilitated by essay writing (p. 210).

Langer and Applebee (1987) offer a substantial contribution to the research on writing to learn through their book, *How Writing Shapes Thinking.* "What contribution, if any," ask Langer and Applebee (1987, p. 5), "does written language make to intellectual development?" Among their many conclusions are the following

1. Writing activities promote learning better than activities involving only studying or reading.

2. Different kinds of writing activities lead students to focus on different kinds of information.

3. In contrast to short-answer responses, which turn information into discrete small pieces, analytic writing promotes more complex and thoughtful inquiry but on a smaller amount of information. (Langer & Applebee 1987 pp. 135–136)

In other words, although writing promotes more focused, complex consideration of the subject matter, the volume of information learned is narrowed. Whereas summary writing and notetaking lead to comprehensive but superficial understandings of the subject matter, analytic writing, by promoting depth rather than breadth, inevitably neglects whatever information was not included in the construction of the essay. Accordingly, teachers need to be aware of the various consequences of the forms and contexts of writing they introduce in the classroom.

An accurate indication of the status and flavor of the writing to learn movement during the 1980s comes from *The Journal Book,* edited by Toby Fulwiler (1987a; see also Fulwiler, 1987b). Drawing from a vast cadre of language scholars, including Lev Vygotsky (1962), James Moffett (1968, 1981), Britton (1970), Britton et al. (1975), Emig (1971,

1977), and Peter Elbow (1973, 1982), the 48 authors of this anthology celebrate the role of journal writing in the learning lives of their students, in disciplines ranging from English, philosophy, art, and music to political science, history, chemistry, and physics. Although under-theorized, this collection stands as one of the most cited writing to learn resources among teachers of writing.

Nothing Begins with N, an anthology of 16 articles edited by Pat Belanoff, Peter Elbow, and Sheryl Fontaine (1991), provides a response to the lack of research and reflection on freewriting. Although the articles range considerably in topic and method, from James Pennebaker's experimental study of the effects of freewriting on the emotional states of writers to Sheridan Blau's investigation of the process of "invisible writing," many of the authors address in some way the possible connections between freewriting and thinking in both school and non-school settings.

To develop a more nuanced understanding of how journal writing might support learning, Susan Peck MacDonald and Charles Cooper (1992) studied the effects of prolonged dialogic (student-structured) and academic (teacher-structured) journal writing on the quality and sophistication of final-exam essays in a Chinese literature course. The students who kept academic journals outperformed the students who kept dialogic journals, as well as those who kept no journal, on the three measures of essay quality and sophistication considered. Those students who kept dialogic journals based on a more open ended prompt calling for personal response, in fact, performed more poorly than students who did no journal writing at all. This study is a cautionary tale for composition teachers who uncritically advocate dialogic journals across the curriculum: "If we grant that students have some stake in being able to see things as their professors see them," conclude MacDonald and Cooper (p. 154), "our research suggests that, left to their own devices, students may fail to perceive the issues [pertinent to the professor], perceive them in ways different from their professors, or remain at too low a level of abstraction."

Similar caution is also suggested by Ackerman's 1993 review of thirty-five studies of writing to learn activities. He found the results inconclusive because of poor research designs, mismatches between the writing activities and the measures of learning, and predispositions of the researchers of find positive affects. He found the evidence particularly uneven when it came to how the interpretive-meaning making aspects of writing impacted traditional measures of memory recall. His conclusion is that there must be a better understanding of what kind of writing fosters what kind of learning. A general predisposition towards discovery writing as a general and unqualified good needs to be replaced with a more precise investigation of how specific kinds of activities support specific forms of learning.

Discipline Specific Approaches

In recent years, the writing to learn movement has continued to migrate from general approaches to discipline-specific studies of the relation between writing and learning (see Gardner & Fulwiler, 1998). Lamenting the writing skills of her computer science students, Janet Hartman (1989) incorporated five types of the microtheme, "an essay so short that it can be typed on a single five-by-eight inch note card," into her data structures course as a way to encourage robust learning of data structures as well as to practice effective communication among peers. These activities included summarizing articles, generating and articulating theses based on data, and explaining the behavior of a novel algorithm to a peer, all of which, according to Hartman, challenged students to approach, learn, and explain the complexities of the subject matter in new and thought-provoking ways.

In biology, Robert Cannon (1990) incorporated personal journals into his courses on general microbiology, virology, and immunology as a way to improve his students' writing skills as well as to encourage closer interaction with the class material through frequent free-form writing tasks. Although his WAC-based courses initially attracted significantly fewer students than his traditional courses, within a few years the course enrollments restabilized at normal levels, and his students were overwhelming positive about the journal writing experience, which enabled them to approach the material in their own way while providing assurance to Cannon that the students were, in fact, engaging the required texts. "More importantly," notes Cannon, "I am convinced that students are learning more about Microbiology, Virology and Immunology, because they are spending more time thinking about the discipline through their writing" (p. 157). Another early use of journal writing within the engineering curriculum is recounted by Selfe & Arbabi (1983, 1986).

In physics, Audet, Hickman, and Dobrynina (1996) studied the effects of computerized journals, or "learning logs," on advanced high-school students. Besides fostering a positive interpersonal environment that flattened the hierarchy of classroom authority, the learning logs highlighted and encouraged the negotiation of scientific sense-making as well as the co-construction of knowledge. Journals have also played a role in sociology: In Sociology, Frances Coker and Allen Scarboro (1990) introduced the "free write," both open ended and focused, in their sociology courses as a way to generate discussion and create a sharing interpersonal environment. However, the journals were also used as repositories of thoughts, cognitive and affective responses to readings, as well as rough drafts of course papers. Coker, in particular, noted encouraging results: "Students are showing earlier a more marked sophistication in delving into classical sociological theory. They are more willing to risk making interpretations and receiving criticisms in class, are working more closely with the texts they read, and are more willing to challenge each other, the instructor, and the sources they read. Finally, they write more cleanly, more clearly, and more persuasively than previous students" (p. 219).

In nursing, Kathleen Cowles, Donna Strickland, and Beth Rodgers (2001) introduced journal writing as an effective invention technique to help students prepare for a personal nursing philosophy paper due at the end of the course. In previous years, professors were disappointed by the "brief and perfunctory" nature of the philosophies they received. So Cowles, Strickland, and Rodgers gave their students the last 10 minutes of each class to reflect on the week's classroom and clinical experiences and to make notes about how these experiences might help them form their personal philosophies. The results were unanimously positive:

> The outcome of this strategy was comparable to the results obtained in other courses in which WTL [writing to learn] strategies were used in that the evolving nursing philosophies were far superior to those written by other groups without this continuing experience. (Cowles, Strickland, & Rodgers 2001, p. 365)

Likewise, Angela Gillis (2001) found that journal writing helped nursing students at her institution articulate their own values and epistemological assumptions, thus enabling them to exert more conscious control over their practices. Journal writing also provided students with an inexpensive, time-efficient process for integrating classroom and clinical experiences into a systematic whole. Gillis recommended the following guidelines for students "embarking on the journaling process":

- Establish a clear statement of purpose for the use of journaling in your clinical learning experience that is mutually agreed on by you, the writer, and the reader.

- Begin the use of journal entries with your first clinical experience.

- Make regular journal entries so that the progress of your learning can be traced.

- Immediacy should be a guiding principle in your journaling. Record entries either concurrently with the learning experience or as soon as possible after completion of your clinical experience.

- A spiral notebook is the most useful took to keep together a progressive record of your learning.

- Use a double-entry format with the left-column reserved for descriptive narrative and the right column designated for reflection and critical analysis...

- Maintain a section on personal learning objectives that you evaluate on a regular basis [. . .]

- Keep a section to record new questions or challenges that have emerged for you as a result of the clinical experience and the process of journal writing. (Gillis, 2001, p. 54)

In statistics, Sandra Sgoutas-Emch and Camille Johnson (1998) explored the relationship between journal writing and student anxiety toward statistics (for writing to learn in statistics see also Beins, 1993; Dunn, 1996). Encouraged by work on therapeutic writing by Pennebaker and Beall (1986) and Rabinor (1991), Sgoutas-Emch and Johnson (1998) conducted an experiment with 44 undergraduate students in two statistics classes in which they studied the effect of journal writing on students' reported levels of anxiety surrounding statistics course content. Although journal writing offered no indication of improvement in attitudes toward statistics itself, the authors did find a statistically significant decrease in anxiety toward the content among those who kept a journal. Journal writing, concluded Sgoutas-Emch and Johnson (1998), "may be an effective tool in curtailing feelings and responses to exams in statistics and possibly other related courses" (p. 49).

With the move toward discipline-specific writing studies has come increased interest in other genres, such as the experimental article, scientific biography, and the laboratory report, and how the genre-specific literate practices of various disciplines might shape the attendant cognitive processes of students (Keys, 1999; Kelly &Takao, 2002; Kelly & Bazerman, 2003). Last, Leona English (2001) has begun to raise ethical concerns about students being required to disclose and blend their professional and personal lives in the pages of mandatory journals, especially given the inadequate support services available in the typical university classroom. With mandatory journal writing also comes the increased responsibility of ensuring students' rights to privacy and confidentiality, a responsibility that English suggests teachers take very seriously before implementing journal writing in the classroom.

6

Rhetoric of Science, Rhetoric of Inquiry, and Writing in the Disciplines

A third cluster of approaches to writing across the curriculum arises from various groups of researchers, theorists, and critics who have examined the specialized languages of the disciplines, professions, and sciences. This examination has been motivated by several different professional positions, goals, and assumptions—including disciplinary self-examination, postmodern critique of scientific authority, rhetorical critiques of epistemology, and first and second language instructional concern for the specialized forms of writing students must gain competence in. These inquiries have gone under various names— Rhetoric of Science, Rhetoric of Inquiry, Writing in the Disciplines, and English for Specific Purposes. Collectively, however, these differently motivated and framed inquiries contribute to a common picture of writing practices in the various disciplines and the relation of those processes to the production and use of disciplinary knowledge. They help us understand how different disciplines construct knowledge through different textual forms, and the kinds of challenges students must meet when learning to write within their chosen fields. They thereby provide a more precise focus for write-to-learn pedagogies by identifying the specific forms of disciplinary writing with the kinds of knowledge and analytical tasks the discipline requires of students.

The Politics of Academic Knowledge—
Anthropology's Self-Examination

Anthropology has had long awareness of the role of symbols (for example, Lévi-Strauss, 1975), language (Sapir, 1949), and communicative practices in the formation of cultures. It has also had long interest in the role of language and language practices in the distribution and attribution of power, and it also has had some small awareness of the processes by which work is assembled and texts produced (Bateson, 1958, or the parody "Body Ritual among the Nacirema" (Miner, 1956) often reprinted in freshman anthologies). However, in the late 1970s these issues came together in a reflexive examination of the way anthropological ethnography was written to create particular forms of authority and knowledge from the perspective of dominant western culture. Several articles around 1980 (Crapanzano, 1976, 1977; Clifford 1980, 1983; Marcus 1980a, 1980b; Marcus & Cushman, 1982) foregrounded the role of writing in the making of ethnographic knowledge. Further, several self-conscious experiments in reflexive writing attempted to put this awareness into practice by creating new forms of ethnography (Geertz 1973, 1976, 1980; Crapanzano, 1980; Rosaldo 1980). Because of the discipline's long practice in looking at the relations of language and culture and its cosmopolitan perspective, when the lens was turned on their own knowledge producing practice, the scrutiny and debate were intense. The critique took on rapid momentum and great force—focusing on the production, role, meanings, cultural authority, and power relations instantiated in the ethnography.

The discussion eventuated in a 1984 conference (Marcus & Clifford, 1985), and a consequent volume, *Writing Culture* (Clifford & Marcus, 1986), which has become widely cited as a central work in anthropology's reflection on its rhetorical practices. In one of the chapters of the volume, Mary Louise Pratt examines the ethnographer's self-portrayal as an authoritative investigator, particularly in relation to the opening scene of arrival in the exotic locale. Renato Rosaldo considers how the pastoral mode of ethnography both suppresses and reveals the interplay of power and knowledge by allowing the ethnographic narrator "to enjoy relations suffused with a tender courtesy that appears to transcend inequality and domination." Nonetheless, "the figures of the inquisitor and the fieldworker still haunt the authors" (Rosaldo, 1986, p. 97). James Clifford analyzes the narrative allegories of ethnographies, as they both evoke metaphorically familiar narratives and freight the narratives with allegorical meanings about the human condition. Stephen Tyler finds in ethnographies postmodern performances of the occult. Asad and Rabinow in their chapters consider ethnographies' relations to the western academic audiences for which they are produced, forming a textual representation of other cultures.

Geertz, in a 1988 volume *Works and Lives,* views a number of ethnographic classics as pieces of writing, produced by the particular writing habits and situations of their eminent authors. In 1989, Spencer provides a useful review of the discussion to that point. In the same year, Roth finds this reflective examination of ethnography less epistemologically consequential than others have found it; his challenge is followed by a number of responses by some of the key authors in this project, to form a pointed symposium (Roth, 1989). Sanjek's 1990 collection *Fieldnotes* examines the centrality, mythology, and detailed practices of making fieldnotes and their role in the production of anthropological knowledge.

As a result of this period of intense anthropological self-scrutiny, ethnographies have taken on new forms. Among other concerns, new ethnographies exhibit awareness of the stories they construct, sensitivity to the relation with the informants and local people who provide information, consciousness of the traps of considering "the other," and attempts to contend with the systems of authority and domination that support professional anthropology. Also new ethnographies exhibit awareness of the changing global environment, which brings all cultures into contact with each other and reveals all societies as always undergoing transformation. Part of this awareness that no society is an isolated exotic other is the development of the multi-sited ethnography, discussed by Marcus (1995).

The Social Location and Purposes of Academic Writing—Sociology's Rhetoric

The earliest work to explore the rhetorical dimension of sociological scholarship appeared in the 1970s. Sociologist Joseph Gusfield (1976) used rhetoric to examine the knowledge produced in his own field and to develop a reflexive stance towards sociological knowledge as produced for social purposes within social circumstances. In his "Literary

Rhetoric of Science," he challenged the long-held belief that language serves merely an ornamental function in the production of knowledge by analyzing an influential research paper on drunk driving through the critical lens of Kenneth Burke's (1945) pentad. There he presents the development of knowledge as a social drama, beginning with the very definition of certain issues as social problems, requiring research to seek socially desirable answers. Although the research emerges as part of a social drama, the research papers are written, he notes, in the passive voice, effectively removing the author and creating the perception of objectivity. Agency is then attributed to the research methods, Gusfield notes, through personification, thereby seeming to provide the audience a privileged access to "external reality [which does] [...] the persuading" (Gusfield, 1976, p. 20). "The writer must persuade the audience that the results of the research are *not* literature, are *not* a product of the style of presentation. The style of nonstyle is itself the style of science" (Gusfield, 1976, p. 17). This analysis of the historically located rhetorical character of social knowledge sets the stage for his investigation of social problems research in his book, *The Culture of Public Problems: Drinking-Driving and the Symbolic Order* (Gusfield, 1981).

An additional interesting study of sociological writing is James Bennett's *Oral History and Delinquency: The Rhetoric of Criminology*, which considers the historical conditions under which sociology turns from other modes of inquiry toward oral history (1981). Through a detailed study of major texts in the history of criminology, he finds that when industrialization leads to growth of complex urban societies, oral histories serve to explain and make meaningful the plight of lower class delinquent youth to middle class publics. The complex urban societies also lead to an increase of individualism at the same time freedom-restricting criminal punishments replace traditional communal values and controls. This tension makes for compelling personal stories. The emergence of such stories, however, also requires audiences who are unfamiliar with the lower classes without being repelled by them, ready to believe reports of lower-class life and be persuaded by their cause. Similarly, such stories need to find their champions in criminologist story tellers who identify with the people they report on, who are offended by hypocrisy, and who themselves are somewhat socially marginal sociologists to demonstrate that scientific papers were argumentative, and not direct and unmediated representations of the "facts" of the laboratory.

Richard Harvey Brown in *A Poetic for Sociology* systematically examines the role of aesthetics in creating persuasive sociological texts. In particular, he examines point of view, metaphor, and irony as though sociological texts were novels. In the course of examining how a variety of influential sociological texts work, he concludes that these texts rely on a "relationship between logic and feeling, between science and art" (221). In consequent books Brown (1987; 1989; 1992) extends his inquiry into unconventional and individually creative elements of knowledge formation in the social sciences. Paul Atkinson in a similar vein examines the narrative construction of sociological ethnography in a wide range of sociological texts in *The Ethnographic Imagination* (1990). He particularly attends to the construction of authority, the representation of characters and social action. In a later book, *Understanding Ethnographic Texts* (Atkinson, 1992), he considers how the complexity of life becomes represented within sociological ethnography, including the role of fieldnotes and recording devices. Van Maanen's *Tales of the Field: On Writing Ethnography* (1988) also examines sociological ethnographic writing (see also Van Maanen, *Representation in Ethnography,* 1995). Finally, the sociologist Howard Becker has written an influential guide to *Writing in the Social Sciences,* which reveals the perspective of a major working sociologist on what is really important in sociological writing (Becker, 1986). A follow up book on ethnographic technique, *Tricks of the Trade* (1998), also contains much insight into sociological writing.

The Rhetoric of Economics and the Rhetoric of Inquiry

The rhetoric of inquiry movement was developed by a number of practicing scholars in the social sciences (with a core group at the University of Iowa) who were interested in the rhetorical practices of their own fields so as to open up the range and character of inquiry and knowledge making. They largely felt that standardized forms of argument in their fields hid their narrowness of perspective, delegitimized other important lines of inquiry, and obscured important issues that needed discussion. In 1985, Deirdre McCloskey's critique of neoclassical economics in *The Rhetoric of Economics* joined the question of rhetoric and epistemology within mainstream economic thought. The overarching iconoclastic thesis is simple: economics is rhetorical. Like mathematics, physics, and biology, economics is "a persuasive realm where the work [is] done by human argument, not godlike Proof" (McCloskey, 1985, p. xii). After criticizing modernism and introducing a small cadre of rhetorical concepts to her readers, McCloskey moves toward an understanding of economics in literary and rhetorical terms. The book examines the reasons economists believe in their flagship theorem—the law of demand—and argues that only the first three reasons are scientific, while the remaining eight are artistic and literary. Other chapters illustrate the rhetoric of economics through case studies of Paul Samuelson, Gary Becker, Robert Solow, John Muth, and Robert Fogel. Another chapter demonstrates how one young economist, Ronald Coase, appealed to a sort of Euclidean rhetoric of axiom, fact, and proof to compensate for his junior status and unknown reputation within the field. Yet all of McCloskey's chapters work toward a common thesis: old-fashioned notions of scientific method do little to demonstrate the assent of economic claims within the field; instead, economists rely substantially on rhetoric—on creative analogies, thought experiments, aesthetic predilections for symmetry, quantification, metaphysical propositions, and authority—to persuade their readers of the veracity of their claims. That language constitutes rather than clothes economic knowledge, that rhetoric should replace the failed modernist methodology, and that new students of economics would benefit from a rhetorical awareness of their own field: these are the central themes of McCloskey's influential book.

Before McCloskey there had in fact been some other economists who were developing awareness of the role of language and argument in their field. Nobel laureate George Stigler (1982) provides one of the earliest direct gestures toward rhetorical awareness in economics through his anthology, *The Economist as Preacher and Other Essays*. In "Textual Exegesis as a Scientific Problem," for example, Stigler addresses the difficulty of interpreting a text that contains inconsistent passages. Rejecting the common practice of reconciling passages based on cursory similarities, Stigler encourages economists to adopt a more meaningful evaluation of each passage in question based on (1) its "consistency with the main analytical conclusions of the system of thought under conviction," a concept he calls the principle of scientific exegesis, or (2) its consonance with the author's underlying "style of thought," which he calls the principle of personal exegesis (Stigler, 1982, p. 69). It is a short lesson in reading and interpreting economics that Stigler has in mind, perhaps one of the first in the history of modern economic discourse.

Later essays in Stigler's collection also focus on discourse practices but from a more sociological perspective. In "The Pattern of Citation Practices in Economics," for example, Stigler examines a variety of citation practices in economic discourse from 1885 to 1969 and concludes that (1) successful economics scholarship quickly becomes embedded within the general corpus of science and stripped of its citational linkages back to particular authors or works, and (2) the quantity of an economist's work plays a minor role in how often he or she is cited. In "The Literature of Economics," Stigler focuses on the literature of normal economics (in the Kuhnian sense) and concludes, quite remarkably, that (1) adverse empirical evidence is not a decisive factor in a theory's decline, and (2) roughly two-thirds of the published economic literature adds nothing to economic theory or findings.

Although Arjo Klamer's (1984) *Conversations with Economists* highlights the argumentative element of economics, it took McCloskey's (1985) *Rhetoric of Economics* to propel the rhetoric debate into mainstream economics discourse, touching off a heated debate concerning methodology and argument in economics. Typical of the work done in this vein is the fourth volume of *Economics and Philosophy,* published in 1988, in which four economic methodologists respond to McCloskey's work with varying degrees of contempt. In "How to Combine Rhetoric and Realism in the Methodology of Economics," Maki (1988), for example, mildly scolds McCloskey for muddling multiple conceptions of realism under the single term; Maki then proceeds, in seeming support of McCloskey's main thesis, to differentiate among various forms of realism as a way to approach the concept of a rhetoric-with-realism more successfully in economics. On the other hand, Rosenberg (1988) vehemently rejects McCloskey's entire platform; for Rosenberg, by attempting to reduce economics to a mere "genre" of literature, in which reality and knowledge need not exist, McCloskey's work is best read as a "Sophistic invitation to complacency about economics and an attempted seduction of the discipline into irrelevancy" (Rosenberg, 1988, p. 130). Economists, not philosophers, according to Rosenberg, have much to fear from McCloskey's disillusioned work.

In 1994, McCloskey published *Knowledge and Persuasion in Economics,* a full-scale philosophical response to her critics. Drawing from 20th century philosophers of science such as Popper, Ayer, Quine, Lakatos, Rorty, and Kuhn), McCloskey reaffirms the position she sketched a decade earlier. In the preface to *Knowledge and Persuasion,* she repeats the simple message, so misunderstood by her colleagues: "Let me say it again: the people like Arjo Klamer, Roy Weintraub, and me who want to see economics as 'rhetorical' are not advocating flowery speech or the abandonment of mathematics. We are advocating the study of how economists actually persuade each other and the world" (McCloskey, 1994, p.xv). McCloskey also pursued the role of narrative in economic reasoning (1990) and of gender in economic forms of argument (1996). Conversations along these philosophical or methodological lines, instigated by McCloskey's *Rhetoric of Economics,* continue (Amariglio, 1990; Benton, 1990; Heilbroner, 1990; Klamer & McCloskey, 1995; Rossetti, 1992; Samuels, 1990).

But not all of the discussion incited by McCloskey's book is philosophical. The second strand of work following *Rhetoric of Economics* takes on the task of rhetorically analyzing master texts and popular textbooks in economics. Tony Dudley-Evans and Willie Henderson's (1990) *The Language of Economics,* an edited collection of a half-dozen analyses of economic discourse, provides an early example of this scholarship. In "Dancing on Air," for example, Mary Mason analyzes a short passage from an economics textbook in terms of the concreteness and abstractness of its language. In "The Textbook Presentation of Economic Discourse," Arjo Klamer (1990) provides a rhetorical reading of the introductory chapters of 12 editions of Paul Samuelson's textbook, *Economics.* Some works, such as Roger Backhouse, Tony Dudley-Evans, and Willie Henderson's (1993) *Economics and Language* and David George's (1990) "The Rhetoric of Economics Texts," continue along this line of contemporary inquiry, while other scholars, such as Bazerman (1993) and Brown (1994), have undertaken rhetorical examinations of the classic work of Adam Smith.

The rhetoric of inquiry movement gained group visibility in the social sciences beyond economics with the publication *The Rhetoric of the Human Sciences* (Nelson, Megill & McCloskey, 1987), based on a 1984 University of Iowa Humanities Symposium. This collection of 22 essays by economists, historians, sociologists, anthropologists, philosophers, rhetoricians, mathematicians, and political scientists illus-

trates some of the rhetorical dimensions of scholarship ranging from
theology to history to mathematics. While the motives and perspectives of the several authors varied, an underlying thesis remained the
same, echoing Gusfield's then-decade-old critical perspective against
those who would remove the substance of disciplinary knowledge from
rhetoric, leaving rhetoric with at best an ornamental function. Rather,
those who pursue the rhetoric of inquiry notice rhetorical purposes
in the quixotic attempt to make social sciences appear to be objective
inquiries: protecting the veracity of findings from tainted ideology or
potential collusion and making apparently untainted findings speak
for themselves on the pages of scholarly texts. Rhetoric of inquiry takes
as its starting point that all scholarship—from biology to theology—is
argument. Neither the facts of history nor the proofs of mathematics
speak for themselves. Instead, historians and mathematicians must do
the speaking, and the sooner we begin to recognize this rhetorical dimension in our scholarship, the sooner we can gain conscious control
over our rhetorical decisions and thus improve the quality of our work.
The work of disciplinary self-examination through a rhetorical lens
continues to be carried out by *Poroi,* a center established at the University of Iowa, which now publishes an electronic journal *Poroi,* available
at <http://inpress.lib.uiowa.edu/poroi/>.

A few other publications provide interesting perspectives on disciplinary writing in fields whose writing is less frequently examined.
Personal Effects: The Social Character of Scholarly Writing (Holdstein
& Bleich, 2001) presents a number of reflections on the personal in
scholarly writing, particularly in the humanities. A. J. Soyland's *Psychology as Metaphor* examines through a series of case studies the role
of metaphor in the disciplinary construction of such concepts as memory, development, emotion, IQ, and mind. Although a wide range of
psychological literature is covered in each domain, the attempt is not
to create a comprehensive account of the debates of the field, but rather
to highlight a particular aspect of representational and rhetorical process in each case. Particularly interesting is the book's analysis of the
way the metaphor of the promissory note is used to warrant research
approaches that have yet to provide the results that would both establish the validity and value of the approach. Finally, *Writing and Revising the Disciplines* (Monroe, 2002) presents personal narratives by a
number of eminent researchers in a variety of disciplines reflecting on
their writing experiences.

Scientific Knowledge as Humanly Written—Science Studies

Some sociologists, in the specialties of sociology of science and sociology of knowledge, have turned their eyes to the rhetoric of the natural sciences. They were particularly interested in demonstrating that scientific knowledge was socially produced for social purposes, from within social matrixes of beliefs and practices (Kuhn, 1961, 1962, 1996). Karin Knorr-Cetina (1979) argued from a laboratory study that a scientific paper was produced to appeal to audience interests and was not directly descriptive of scientific work. She expanded on this in her 1981 book *The Manufacture of Knowledge*. Her studies echoed the earlier observation of the notable biologist Peter Medawar (1964) that the scientific paper was a fraud because it created an after-the-fact idealized recounting rather than a detailed chronicle of laboratory events with all its mistakes, misturnings, and wastes of time. Other sociologists pursued similar analyses of the rhetorical reconstruction of scientific accounts (Woolgar, 1981; Yearley, 1981; Gilbert, 1977; Gilbert and Mulkay, 1984; Garfinkel, Lynch & Livingston, 1981), the rhetorical character of experimental work and technology (Collins, 1985; Collins & Pinch, 1982), the formation of the boundary between science and the authority of scientific expertise (Gieryn, 1983, 1999), and the role of representation within scientific practice (Lynch & Woolgar, 1990). Other sociologists (Cozzens, 1985; Small, 1978) were interested in the processes by which some claims got codified in the literature through citation practices.

The most influential sociologically based work in the rhetoric of science was Bruno Latour and Steve Woolgar's (1979) *Laboratory Life*. In this anthropological field study of the Salk Institute, Latour and Woolgar examine the process by which scientific statements gain assent and, ultimately, become accepted as facts by the larger scientific community. Central to this process is another process, "literary inscription": According to Latour and Woolgar, the raw materials within the laboratory are quickly transformed into symbolic currency by the scientists through the routine activities of labeling, coding, and classifying. The materials are further "inscribed" when the scientists subject them to various devices, such as scales, spectrometers, and bioassays, which produce a still more focused symbolic representation of the materials, in the form of graphs, charts, and tables of numbers. At each stage of this literary inscription process, explain Latour and Woolgar, all previous activities are quickly forgotten; all that matters is the latest symbolic representation, which ultimately gets sent to the office section of the laboratory for incorporation into their primary product: the scientific paper. Latour elaborates the analysis of how technologists and scientists enlist allies through rhetorical means in his 1987 book *Science in Action*. Woolgar, along with a number of other sociologists of science, reflexively applied their findings to their own practices (Woolgar, 1988; Mulkay, 1985; Potter & Wetherall, 1987).

Historians of science, by examining crucial moments in the formation of modern science and the way science has been embedded in local belief and practice, also began to question the authority of scientific writing that represents itself as a historical, non-rhetorical, and disinterested. Steven Shapin and Simon Schaffer in the *Leviathan and the Air Pump* (1985) examine an important juncture of seventeenth century science when one form of argument based on material demonstration before socially credible witnesses that obscured its ideological assumptions (associated with Robert Boyle) was preferred over a more overtly politically grounded mode of argument associated with Thomas Hobbes. Shapin in a later book, *Social History of Truth* (1994), examines the social and ideological basis of trust in particular individuals upon which the credibility of scientific claims began to depend. Schaffer (1994) in an essay examines the rhetorical character of self evidence. Peter Dear (1985) has also examined the mid-seventeenth century moment when the Royal Society seemingly eschewed argument by privileging demonstration over words; he found both large verbal argument in attempting to create the non-rhetorical impression and in continuing a tradition of argument over claims. Dear (1987) also examines the shift from scholastic argument where multiple recurrences and typicality served as empirical proof to the form of argument in modern science where accounts of unusual single events began carrying major epistemic weight. Similarly, he has examined the rhetorical contrast between forms of seventeenth century scientific argument in Catholic countries where unique occurrences were attributable to miracles and were thus not taken into account in scientific explanations and Protestant countries where unique events not only had to be included within comprehensive theories but could serve as strong evidence because they revealed unusual aspects of nature (Dear, 1990). Mario Biagioli (1993) in *Galileo, Courtier* examines how Galileo pursued his science, represented his findings, and created his own scientific identity as part of his advancement at court. Other historians of science examining rhetoric in the formation of science at different moments of history include Jan Golinski (1992), David Gooding (1990), Larry Stewart (1992), Adrian Johns (1998), and Mary Slaughter (1982). See also the collection *The Literary Structure of Scientific Argument* (Dear, 1991).

Rhetoric of Science

Rhetoricians also entered into the examination of scientific writing during the same period. John Angus Campbell (1975) in "The Polemical Mr. Darwin" finds Darwin to be a brilliant arguer. Darwin's persuasiveness starts with his presenting the facts he noted in his travels as obviously true. By then arguing methodically and inductively from those facts, Darwin appealed to his audience's Baconian belief that "close, dogged observation rather than abstract theorizing was the principle key to scientific advance" (Campbell, 1975, p. 378). Equally important, by proceeding via analogy from the image of a domestic breeder in chapter one to the idea of natural selection in chapter four, Darwin advanced his revolutionary pronouncement within the guise of household Victorian terms. The strategy was effective, according to Campbell, for "so skillfully does Darwin interweave traditional and revolutionary elements that the Victorian reader may here be unaware of the extent to which Darwin's traditional deference to nature concealed a revolution in the conventional conception of nature" (p. 382). Like the sociologists of Gusfield's study, Darwin effectively deployed the rhetorical style of non-style, convincing his readers that the veracity of his *Origins* lay somewhere beyond style, somewhere beyond persuasion. For more of his work on the rhetoric of Charles Darwin, see Campbell (1974, 1986, 1989).

In rhetoric, Campbell's essays were joined by Weimer's (1977) and Overington's (1977) philosophical essays, which argued in general theoretical terms for a nonjustificational approach to science and rhetoric. Alan Gross (1984, 1985, 1988), in a series of essays and analyses of scientific texts, followed suit in arguing for the rhetoricity of scientific writing and advocating of relativism as an intellectually respectable position and the creation of the rhetoric of science as a legitimate academic discipline. In his *Rhetoric of Science* (Gross, 1990), he advances a more epistemologically radical claim: it is not that science has a rhetorical dimension, but that science is, "without remainder," a rhetorical endeavor. "A complete rhetoric of science," challenges Gross, "must avoid this accusation: after analysis, something unrhetorical remains" (Gross, 1990, p. 33).

The philosopher of science Shea (1972) had already analyzed Galileo's arguments in *Dialogue of the Two World Systems* to show that Galileo's form of argument was a rational procedure. Pera (1994; Pera & Shea, 1991) continued to advance the defense of scientific argument as authoritative and creating solid epistemic grounds for science. The philosopher Steve Fuller (1988, 1993) on the other hand wholeheartedly accepted the idea that science was historical and rhetorical, and that it was important for the public to understand this to allow for full citizen participation in setting science policy.

More concretely, Laurance Prelli (1989) examined the role of rhetorical invention, the rhetorical concept of stasis (or the joining point of arguments), and topoi (or lines of argument) in a number of scientific texts. Jeanne Fahnestock (1999) has similarly examined the role of rhetorical figures in science, such as antithesis, incremental series, and repetition. These figures serve as forms of thought as well as expression. Another rhetorical anthology of interest is Herb Simons' (1990) *The Rhetorical Turn,* which examines the rhetorical dimension of texts in science, politics, and philosophy, among other fields.

The rhetoric of science movement was opened to further critique by Dilip Parameshwar Gaonkar (1990). According to Gaonkar, rhetoric, insofar as it is informed by the Aristotelian and Ciceronian traditions, is a productive art, concerned with generating and presenting speeches in the *agora*. It is not sufficient to be used as a theory of text interpretation, as a "hermeneutic," as the rhetoric of inquiry movement demands. Second, this productive nature implies a strategic model of communication, which places a disproportionate portion of agency on the shoulders of a perpetually intentional author. Third, because the categories of rhetoric are abstract, rhetoric is "thin" from an analytic perspective. In other words, because terms such as the *topoi* or the tripartite scheme of *logos-pathos-ethos* elude precise definitions, they lack contestability. Consequently, without a more systematic or "deepened" (Gaonkar, 1997, p. 33) set of analytic terms, claims from such studies should not be classified as knowledge. Goankar's critique became the center of a symposium, *Rhetorical Hermeneutics* (Gross

& Keith, 1997), which included responses from Steve Fuller, Deirdre McCloskey, Michael Leff, Carolyn Miller, and others. It is worth noting, however, that Goankar does not engage the analysis of the rhetoric of science coming from writing studies, as presented below—which include approaches that are distinctly more production oriented, that strongly locate text production within historical and social circumstances as well as traditions of communication, and that are empirically grounded.

Another distinct tradition of comment on the rhetoric and literary character of scientific writing comes from scientists and science journalists who are interested in explaining the vitality and thought of science as realized in its writing. This follows a long tradition of appreciation and anthologies of scientific writing (before Darwin, etc.). David Locke's *Science as Writing* (1992) explores essayistically such issues as science's affinity to literature, modes of scientific representation, personalization within scientific writing, rhetorical argument in science, and the reality of writing. Similarly, Scott Montgomery (1996) considers issues of jargon in science politics of scientific translation, and the history of scientific language. In a series of essays, Roald Hoffman (1988, 2002; Hoffman & Laszlo, 1991) has examined how modes of representation in chemistry grow out of different fundamental theories of the nature of chemical matter and processes

Critical studies of science, particularly concerned with gender and race issues, also looked to a study of the role of scientific forms of writing and forms of scientific expression in both fostering genred and racialized knowledge and in favoring particular kinds of participation and participants. Evelyn Fox Keller's biography, for example, considers how Barbara McClintock's style of work constituted "a different language." (Keller, 1983),. One of the key themes is the role of situatedness and experience within disciplinary writing; a related theme is the relation between epistemology and expression (Tuana, 1989; Duran, 1998; Keller, 1985; Traweek, 1988; Treichler, 2000; Treichler, Cartwright & Penley, 1998; Harding, 1986, 1987, 1993, 1998). Finally, *Natural Eloquence: Women Reinscribe Sciences* (Gates & Shtier, 1997) presents a number of analyses of women's alternative styles of science writing.

Writing and Language Focused Approaches
to Writing in the Disciplines

Simultaneous with these studies, scholars in writing across the curriculum and technical writing began more intensive investigation of writing in various disciplinary and professional domains. Unlike the critical aim of much of the other work on the rhetoric of sciences, the aim of these writing scholars was pedagogical. By better understanding the literate activity of science, they hoped to be able to improve instruction in scientific writing and provide tools for students and other writers to better understand what they were doing.

The first essay to clearly set out the agenda of investigating the character and role of disciplinary texts was Charles Bazerman's "What Written Knowledge Does" (1981). This comparative analysis of prominent articles in biochemistry, sociology, and literary studies considers how they argue within differing landscapes of authorial role, audience stance, object studied, and disciplinary literatures. The relationships among these four elements represented in the text and how the texts stand in relation to disciplinary community and practice make each text distinctive, "different moves in different games" (p. 387).

To better understand the distinctiveness of those ways of knowing advanced within articles reporting scientific experiments, Bazerman explored the historical development and contemporary use of the genre of experimental article. *Shaping Written Knowledge: the Genre and Activity of the Experimental Article in Science* (1988; available online at http://wac.colostate.edu/books/bazerman_shaping/) situates the scientific article within its historical and social context and casts communicative success in the light of making effective literate choices in response to local historical circumstances. He found that the invention of scientific journals in 1665 created new argumentative dynamics within new structures of scientific community, making the earlier forms of scientific communication in books and letters less persuasive. Particularly influential in this early period was Newton's concern to create a more mathematical form of argument. The form of scientific articles rapidly evolved over the first century and a half to take on much of the modern shape by 1800, except for modern forms of reference and citation which didn't mature until the nineteenth century. In a later study, Bazerman found the origins of reviews of literature and modern citation practices in the late eighteenth century work of

Joseph Priestley (Bazerman, 1994). Priestley's concern to accumulate the collective experience of nature represents a more cooperative collaborative aspect that is as much a part of scientific communication as competitive argument. The new systems of intertextuality were closely tied to Priestley's social views about the collaborative nature of science and the advancement of the human community. The changes in the form of articles were closely tied to changes in the social relations, theoretical developments, and material practices within the various sciences. A more recent study (Atkinson, 1999) tied major changes in the style of seventeenth and eighteenth science to the replacement of a gentlemanly style of self presentation with a more agonistic professional scientific culture. Also, Battalio (1998a) has traced the changing discourse of American ornithology in relation to the professionalization of the field in the nineteenth and twentieth centuries.

As a consequence of this historical evolution of scientific writing, twentieth century scientists reading and writing such articles did so within well structured sets of concerns and goals with relation to the material world, the material and social technology of their laboratories, the intellectual structures of knowledge that evolved within their fields, and their perceived interaction with their colleagues. Articles in one physics specialty became increasingly organized around and embedded within theory as quantum theory became the standard explanatory tool of the field (Bazerman, 1984a, 1988). Physicists read the literature of their specialties through lenses of their own research projects, their estimates of the communal trajectory of their fields, and their evaluations of the approaches and quality of work of particular colleagues as well as their concrete understanding of the phenomena they were studying (Bazerman, 1985, 1988). And one physicist drafted and revised his essays sharply mindful of the epistemic distinctions made in his field and the kinds of critical evaluations his readers were likely to impose given the arguments current in the field. (Bazerman, 1984b, 1988) The most influential vehicle for the importation of the experimental article into the social sciences has been experimental psychology. The genre was transformed and mobilized through the behaviorist theory and epistemology of the leading figures in experimental psychology. This particular interpretation of the experimental article became institutionalized in the various editions of the Publication Manual of the American Psychological Association. (Bazerman, 1987, 1988).

Greg Myers' studies in *Writing Biology* (1990a) track how both research proposals and research articles are socially constructed within review and revision processes, so that the original authors become responsive to the judgments and perceptual frames of their peers in order to gain funding and publication. These processes have consequences for the scope of the claims being made, the theories being invoked, and the kinds of investigations pursued. Myers also considers how scientific presentations for more popular audiences construct narratives of nature rather than narratives of the construction of scientific knowledge. In other publications, Myers has examined how scientists use linguistic devices of politeness (1989) and irony (1990b) in order to soften the confrontational edge of disagreement. He has also examined the function and varying styles of reviews of literature essays by eminent scientists to reconstruct knowledge, suggest the trajectory of future work, and establish forward looking research programs (Myers, 1991).

Blakeslee (2001) has examined how scientists doing interdisciplinary work have come to know and argue to new audiences. This is an ongoing process of interaction and increasing alignment to the audience over time, rather than simply a one-time analysis to shape the rhetoric of a single text.

A good sampler of the many kinds of analysis of scientific writing that have emerged in recent years can be found in the collection of essays *Understanding Scientific Prose,* edited by Jack Selzer (1993). Each of the fifteen essays in this casebook analyzes a single unusual scientific article by Steven Jay Gould and Richard Lewontin (1979) "The Spandrels of San Marcos and the Panglossian Paradigm." The approaches of the analyses include narrativity, intertextuality, cultural studies, gender studies, reader response, classical rhetoric, and linguistic pragmatics. Stephen Jay Gould provides a final response. Another collection, *Essays in the Study of Scientific Discourse* (1998b), edited by John Battalio, equally testifies to the diversity in approaches, methods, and purposes among those who, for reasons pedagogical, epistemological, or other, find the literate activity of scholarly inquiry of sustaining intellectual interest. An archaeological approach to the discourse surrounding Chronic Fatigue Syndrome, a rhetorical approach to scientific discourse, as well as a statistical analysis of the writings of Joseph Priestly: Another collection, Bazerman and Paradis's (1991) *Textual Dynamics of the Professions* presents 15 in-depth analyses of literate activity in contexts ranging from contemporary biology to medieval letter writing. The diversity of articles examine situatedness of writing processes and the particular ways in which writing is indeed a form of social action and constitutive of social reality. Socially situated approaches to writing have been strongly influenced by genre and activity theory (see Chapter 7); articles on academic writing from this perspective are reviewed in Russell (1997b), which is part of a special issue of *Mind, Culture and Activity* devoted to the Activity of Writing. Another collection taking this perspective is *Writing Selves and Societies* (Bazerman & Russell, 2003).

There have been fewer studies of writing in the humanities and social sciences. Susan Peck MacDonald (1994) has done the most extensive comparative study of writing in the social sciences and humanities. In comparing writing from literary studies, social history, and social psychology, she found that there were systematic relations between the grammatical and lexical features of the texts to the motives and epistemologies—how they frame and investigate problems—of the different fields. She finds greater compactness in theory and problem formulation in the social sciences than in the humanities. The humanities she finds concerned with detailed interpretive representations of their particularized objects of attention, while social sciences tend to be more conceptually driven. She finds these differences both at the level of larger argument structures and detailed sentence-level style structures.

In analyzing the rhetoric of literary studies Fahnestock and Secor (1991) found that literary arguments rely on the topics of paradox, appearance/reality, ubiquity, paradigm, *contemptus mundi,* and complexity.

Lucille McCarthy (1991) has studied the influence of the American Psychiatric Associations manual of mental disorders on the writing of articles in psychiatry, finding that the Diagnostic Statistical Manual has become in essence a charter document, shaping and underlying both research and practice genres in the mental health field. Berkenkotter has extended this work to examine how the DSM has developed out of the biologic tradition of taxonomy and the medical nosology (Berkenkotter, 2001, 2002). Berkenkotter and Ravotas (1997, 1998, 2001, 2002) have examined how that psychiatric language is applied through notes and reports to patients, and how it enters into the dialog with psychiatric clients. Reynolds, Mair, and Fisher (1992) survey the genres within the mental health professions.

Another style of analysis of disciplinary texts has developed in the applied linguistic field of English for Specific Purposes. The research in this field is directed towards finding structures of professional texts that can be used to aid advanced English as a second language learners who have specific disciplinary or professional interests. Swales (1990) and Bhatia (1993) explain the mode of genre analysis used in this field, which seeks to identify a series of rhetorical moves by which content and reasoning is organized in professional texts. The most well known finding in this work is Swales' model of scientific article introductions, which he calls the CARS (or Create A Research Space) model. This model consists of three primary moves: establishing a territory; establishing a niche; and finally occupying that niche. The first move of establishing a territory can be realized by asserting the centrality of a claim, making topic generalizations, and/or reviewing the literature. The second move of establishing a niche may be made by asserting a counter-claim, indicating a gap, raising questions, or continuing a tradition. The final move of occupying a niche can be realized by outlining the purposes of the project at hand or announcing the present research, announcing the principal findings, and finally indicating the structure of the article to follow. Swales (1998) engages another mode of situated text analysis, which he calls textography, by examining the different forms of writing and texts to be found on the three separate floors of a small academic building. Another important work out of the ESP tradition is Kenneth Hyland's (2000) book *Disciplinary Discourses,* which examines both hedging and citation practices. The journal *English For Specific Purposes* carries much of the research in this field. Related work comes from the Structural Functional Linguistics tradition that has developed sensitive linguistic tools for the analysis of texts, including academic and scientific texts (see, for examples, Halliday, 1985; Halliday & Martin, 1993).

7

On-Going Concerns: The Particularity of Disciplinary Discourses

Unity vs. Particularity

One enduring theoretical issue with major implications for evaluation of students and shaping of curricula in academic writing is the degree to which academic writing is the same or different across disciplinary settings. Most people involved in teaching and research in academic writing would agree that there are some features and skills of writing that are generally held in common across all academic settings, most clearly seen in such matters of conventional correctness such as spelling or subject-verb agreement, although they might disagree on whether failure to uniformly adhere to these conventions might characterize the overall literacy of any individual. And most would also agree that writing in each field and at each level of education requires attending to particular formats and adopting particular styles, although again they might well disagree on the value of these practices and the depth of learning required to produce them. The disagreements are fundamentally over the degree and significance of similarity and difference, and therefore on what learning to write in academic settings entails, how any student's competence should be assessed, and how writing should be taught and curricula organized.

The tension between these two points of view is illustrated in a report titled "WPA Outcomes Statement for First-Year Composition," from a steering committee of the Writing Program Administrators. The purpose of the committee was to "articulate a general curricular framework for first-year composition, regardless of institutional home, student demographics, and instructor characteristics" (Steering Committee, 2001, p. 321). In short, the committee was trying to define the disciplinary "what" of first-year comp, a generalized set of fundamentals to be taught across all versions of the introductory course. Yet the document also works from the assumption that good writing is diverse, defined and evaluated variously by both different disciplines and different rhetorical contexts. In an introduction to the document, Kathleen Blake Yancey lists as a benefit that the outcome statement allows WPAs to "argue for the role of genre in first-year composition [...] and for the role that faculty outside of English must play in fostering student literacy" (Steering Committee, 2001, p. 323).

The tension between generalized writing skills and particularized instances of writing is apparent in the bifurcated statement of target outcomes. The outcomes are divided into four sections or areas of focus: Rhetorical Knowledge; Critical Thinking, Reading, and Writing; Process; and Knowledge of Conventions. Each section contains two lists. The first list begins with the universalizing phrase "*By the end of first-year composition, students should...*" and the second list begins with the particularizing phrase "*Faculty in all programs and departments can build on this preparation by helping students learn...*" (p. 321). Thus, while the first list identifies generalized writing skills and knowledge to the composition class, the second list includes faculty from across the university in the continued development of writing ability.

The view of writing as a discipline-specific activity is reinforced in the set of objectives for students and faculty. As outlined by the document, the goals of the composition classroom include both the kinds of skills and knowledge traditionally emphasized in composition classes with a unified view of writing (i.e., students should focus on a purpose), as well as skills and knowledge associated with writing as diversified (i.e., students should use conventions of format and structure appropriate to the rhetorical situation and meet the expectations of disciplinary readers). Other things faculty can pass on to students are how technologies are used to research and communicate in the various disciplines and the "relationships among language, knowledge, and power in their fields" (Steering Committee, 2001, p. 324).

This particular division between generality and particularity, however, would not satisfy a large number of scholars and curricular designers. On one side, pressing for more commonality in instruction, is the long tradition of instruction, textbooks and handbooks that frame writing instruction in terms of a general set of skills and concepts that will consistently direct one towards correct and effective writing. One current manifestation of this tradition of writing as singular and uniform comes from the advocates of what is now being called Academic English, defining a single set of standards for student writing. Of course this is an educationally attractive idea, for insofar as a single core set of teachable language skills can be associated with academic success, clearly those skills should have major curricular focus until such point as students can be demonstrated to have learned them or securely on a path to gain them. Further students might reasonably be held accountable for learning them as well as teachers and system curricula for teaching them, and that the demonstration of such skills would be required for entry to more advanced academic experiences (Scarcella, 2003). Such reasoning often stands behind state curriculum standards for grades K-12 in Language Arts. The identification of such a set of standards for performance, it should be noted, is distinct from the question of how these standards are best taught and learned, directly or indirectly, atomistically or integrated within complex activities.

Another more pedagogically-based version of the unity of writing comes from those who go beyond a performance based notion of unity. Rather than saying "Good writing is good writing," they might say "Good writing is the result of numerous factors—factors which are present in some shape or form and to some degree in all instances of good writing." Rather than claiming that all writing is essentially the same, they might say that the act of writing shares some universal or general principles across various situations. The unity of writing is what allows writers to move successfully between and among various domains and various writing situations. It isn't that all good writing is the same, or even that a good writer can handle all kinds of writing; instead, writers use and must account for a set of essentials that are fairly stable even as they address the particulars of any writing situation.

The earliest rhetoricians, even those who deeply recognized the particularity of writing situations, sought general approaches to framing language. The anonymous sophist who composed the *Dissoi Logoi,* offes a simple general formula: "Everything done at the right time is seemly and everything done at the wrong time is disgraceful" (Sprague, 1972). One must merely decide what is the right time to do something or not do something to achieve seemliness and avoid disgrace. This opens up the issue of differences of situations and styles and forms of presentation, but subsumes them under a general skill that is in the hands of the rhetoric.

Recent theorists and teachers of writing have found unifying principles of writing in the author's relationship to the emerging text. The writer must find his or her personal voice and must claim ownership of the text, for successful writing to result.

The concept of voice is wide-spread in composition pedagogy and is discussed in most writing textbooks. A passage from Donald Murray's (1991) *The Craft of Revision,* in a chapter titled "Re-Write with Voice," will serve to illustrate what is generally meant by voice:

> Now I can play the music of language that will wrap around the words and give them that extra aura of meaning that is the mark of effective writing. It is the music of language that draws the writer to the writing desk and informs the writer of the meanings and feelings that lie within the subject; it is the music of language that attracts and holds the reader and causes the reader to trust and believe the writer; it is the music of language that provides emphasis and clarity." (Murray, 1991, p. 168)

Murray also includes a list of problems that develop when a text has no voice, including lack of emotional engagement and a sense of anonymity in a text.

Ownership is also a common term in contemporary composition pedagogy. Much of the interest in the issue of ownership is associated with Paolo Friere and his American interpreters, such as Ira Shor, Cy Knoblauch, and Lil Brannon. Linda Adler-Kassner (1998) also argues that progressives like Fred Newton Scott and John Dewey saw ownership as an important ingredient in a student's impulse to write. Further, she argues they preferred the essay form, in that it provided a place for students to articulate themselves in the language that is closest to them and their social and cultural setting.

On the other side are those who find great differences in the characteristics and considerations at play in writing in different situations. Their concerns go beyond the response of any piece of writing to some local particulars of the situation and the necessity to meet the formal conventions expected as appropriate to the situation. They argue that the very tasks that writing accomplishes, the means by which it accomplishes it, the considerations that one must address, and the process by which one brings a piece of writing are deeply embedded within differing social arrangements and uses of languages to accomplish manifestly different activities. Thus students are aided most by learning how to understand and participate in specific writing situations, including learning and responding to the local criteria and expectations, as well as strategically deploying task-relevant techniques. In this view the application of general criteria of writing quality and the instruction in general principles and procedures may even be counter-productive because it turns the writer's attention and energy away form noting and responding to the particularity of the situation, task, and means.

Because Writing Across the Curriculum and writing in the disciplines potentially highlights the differences in writing within different academic situations, Bazerman and Russell (1994) consider it challenging the traditional general teachings of rhetoric, that homogenize all rhetorical situations into the oral legal and political institutions that gave rise to classical rhetoric. They note that the medieval art of letter writing began to address the particular rhetorical characteristics of bureaucratic and economic relations enacted through writing, but that these *Ars Dictaminis* remained only a minor by-way on the rhetorical tradition, with little influence on the continuing classical tradition. Similarly in the seventeenth and eighteenth centuries several rhetoricians, including Bacon, Priestley, and Smith, started to develop print-based rhetorics that addressed new social systems of influence, including journalism, literary culture, and the sciences. By 1800, these alternative rhetorics were homogenized into Bellettrism, which formed the ground for literary studies, leaving the rhetorical tradition to remain focused on its traditional concerns of political and legal argumentation. They see the engagements writing across the curriculum makes with the practices of different disciplines as once again opening up inquiry into the specialized tasks of writing. This inquiry into particularities of writing tasks has led them and other scholars to turn towards genre and activity theory as ways of articulating these differences, as we will examine in a following section.

This view of writing as a particular located activity has even led some scholars to argue for the abolition of the general first year college writing course, and make all writing instruction embedded in disciplinary coursework or apprenticeship situations. A number of essays taking this perspective, reviewing the history of the debate, and providing alternatives to generalized composition instruction are collected in Joseph Petraglia's (1995) *Reconceiving Writing, Rethinking Writing Instruction.* Authors in that volume draw on studies in situated cognition and cognitive psychology, pragmatic phenomenology, functional linguistics, as well as activity theory to argue that writing development occurs only within committed engagement to focused organized task environments. They do not believe general instruction in general writing skills to meet general criteria of good writing can elicit the situated engagement and situated decision making that leads to improvement in writing. Bazerman, in a final essay, however, suggests that the first-year writing course can develop as a meaningful site for student writing, addressing the intellectual and personal issues of students entering a particular institution of higher education within a small group of similarly situated people, who can get to know each other and who can respond to each other's writing and concerns. The committed and responsive discussion of matters of personal importance, drawing on the intellectual resources of the university, provides a basis for students to enter into the various other literate interactions they will encounter in the university and beyond.

Genre and Activity Theories

A favored conceptual approach to understanding and researching the diversity of writing has been to consider how genre comes to organize writing and writing processes within differing settings. Writing in different areas is visibly different. A lab report in physics is organized in different ways, reports on different kinds of events, uses different kinds of evidence, and argues for different kinds of points than an analysis of a poem or a paper in history. We recognize these different kinds of writing by calling the different kinds of writing different genres—the lab report, the poetry analysis, the history essay. These highly visible differences marked by well-known genre names both indicate to us the diversity of writing and give us a framework for examining the ranges and distinctions of diversity in writing.

One way to look at genre is to attempt to identify the specific genres people write in and identify the distinctive characteristics of each. Within a fixed domain at one particular historical moment, among users who share a similar orientation towards texts, this can be quite a useful approach. For example, Amy Devitt (1991) found that among tax accountants in the late 1980s there were thirteen well-recognized kinds of letters, memos, and other documents written by professionals that described the full range of texts and work of the profession, which she called the genre set of that profession. Moreover, each of those text-types had specific motives, forms, audiences, styles, and ways of relating to the tax code.

As useful as genre is as a concept and a practical, every-day means of distinguishing kinds of writing, researchers have found that genre is a more slippery category than it first appears. Take the case of the experimental report in science. An article reporting an experiment in a physics journal is noticeably different than one in a chemistry journal, as would be recognized by any practitioner—and particularly anyone attempting to present results to both of the journals. Experimental reports in psychology education might vary even further. Scientists will also recognize and categorize differences between reports from different specialties. Further the characteristics and kinds of articles change historically—the experimental article of the seventeenth century is very far from the one today, having few characteristics of any contemporary journal article. Finally, the characteristics, motives, and goals of a genre change in different educational and professional settings. A high school physics lab report is a far cry from one appearing in a research journal—for many reasons including that a high school student is not expected to be arguing for novel contributions to knowledge, but rather is only demonstrating specific basic kinds of competence in laboratory practice and scientific thinking. Yet, there are some similarities among all these variants and subtypes of experimental article (such as presenting methods and results or observations), even as they might be recognized as very different sorts of communication.

These considerations suggest that the number and kinds of genres proliferate and constantly change, making it hard to establish any fixed and simple taxonomy of text types, or even at what level of generality to identify genres—at the general level of scientific paper or somewhat more specific experimental report or at the much more precise level of introductory college biology lab report incorporating forms from a pre-printed lab manual. Even more troubling for the notion of fixed genre taxonomies, the level at which you might recognize and use genre, or even the categories you might depend on, depend on your level of knowledge and engagement with the area, your socialization into the text-using group, and your particular tasks a t the moment. A college educated person in the humanities who knows little science may see all scientific papers or at least all experimental reports as a single kind, while experts in a scientific specialty may have a much more finely graded set of categories that help them decide what kind of paper they are reading. And even those experts may invoke different categories based on whether they are searching comparable results to support their research or they are looking to determine the current state of thinking about a particular concept or theory. Because of the complex and changing landscape of possible text distinctions and the different genre attributions people may make concerning any text, Bazerman (1988) suggests that we consider genres not as fixed characteristics attaching to particular texts, but as psycho-social recognition categories. That is, genres are what people, as groups and as individuals, recognize them to be. The names people attribute to genres helps strengthen socially shared perception of categories, but there is even some range of meanings and examples people would attribute to a single fixed name. They are social in that the categories become shared through exemplar, instruction, naming, meta-talk and other modes of typification. But they are also individual in that each person's attribution of category affects their orientation towards a text and thus their reading and writing behavior and thought.

The psychosocial processes of categorization or typification, while they may make difficulty for any fixed categories of genres, nonetheless suggest the great power and importance of genre categorization as a process. Genre categorization helps orient and organize individual and group perceptions, thought, and behavior and triggers deeper commonalities than would be suggested by just some text conventions. Devitt's study of tax accountancy letters cited above indicates that genre identified far deeper commonalities of texts than just surface level conventional appearances. Genres gave shape to the interactions, situations, relationships and roles, motives, and even conceptual worlds brought together by the genre. Carolyn Miller's (1984) article "Genre as a Social Act" by defining genres as "typified rhetorical actions based in recurrent situations" brings together the rhetorical tradition of associating genre with particular forms of presentation associated with political and judiciary forums with Schutz's theory of social typification (Schutz, 1967; Schutz & Luckmann, 1973). Schutz argued that we make sense and give order to the potentially infinitely variable everyday world of interactions by the attribution of types to situations and people's behaviors. Through these typifications we make meaning of the every-day life world. These typifications are a kind of self-fulfilling prophecy, for once we interpret our interactional situations and the behavior of others in terms of these types, we behave in ways consistent with these types. These types become shared among people both by how they describe situations and the way that they act that reinforces certain interpretations of meaning. Thus people identifying a certain grouping of people as a class with certain people designated students and others teachers invokes common understandings of what they are doing and how they should behave with each other and draw meaning from each other's behavior. Although participants may bring somewhat different experiences and understandings of what happens and how people behave in a classroom, over time the behaviors and meanings in this classroom become increasingly well-defined and shared, that is typified. Many recent theorists have also found Mikhail Bakhtin's (1986) discussion of genre helpful in elaborating the concept, though Bakhtin's essay on the problem of genre was not available in English until after the framework of this theory of genre was already well developed in ways that extended beyond Bakhtin's interests (Bazerman, in press).

When genre is understood as a kind of typification, we can see how people come to share expectations and assumptions about pieces of writing. Even more we can see how the genres themselves come to shape the entire social interaction, even identifying motives and ways to act (Miller, 1984). The recognition that the sheet of paper handed out by the teacher is an assignment puts an obligation on the students to write in the assigned genre. The range of appropriate (and even resistant) responses is limited as are the motives the students can pursue and enact within the assignment.

By the teacher assigning the paper and by students responding, they are enacting and constituting their roles as teacher and student, reaffirming the typifications that hold the classroom together. We can even say that the entire recognition of a situation requiring action (the rhetorical situation, see Bitzer, 1968) and the defined moment of action is communally shaped and recognized by genre (Bazerman, 1994). Thus in the previous example the rhetorical situation of the student writing is first defined by the assignment genre, with the student have some limited range to reframe the situation to allow novel responses only insofar as the teacher accepts those reframings. Further the situation is temporally initiated by the assignment, and the duration and culmination is set by the assignment deadlines (again depending on the teacher's acceptance of student attempts to redefine the due date). Further the tempo and changing temporal character of the period in between is shaped by the due date. Even more we can see the activity of student and teacher within this period are structured by the assignment situation and the students work to fulfill the obligations of the genre (Bazerman, 1997). Students will inquire about the detailed expectations. Class discussions may prepare students and help raise preliminary ideas. Some class time may be spent on preliminary writing or providing support for the writing. Students may need to go to the library or look back in textbooks to gather materials. Peer groups may be formed to discuss ideas or review manuscript. Again, depending on the genres assigned the entire structure of activities will be changed.

The ways the various texts come together to define situations, provide resources, and serve as interactional contexts for each new piece of writing suggests that genres do not stand alone, but rather exist in systematic relation to one another. Some genres only are timely and meaningful when preceded by another, as a letter to the editor in most cases follows on something previously appearing in the publication, but not too many issues ago. Some genres require responses in other genres, as a blank tax form requires a return of a completed form and a letter of correction in return from the tax agency requires either an acceptance and a check or a further contestation. Some genres rely on the existence of other genres for their composition, as school exams and student answers usually depend on textbooks, other assigned readings, teacher-distributed material, and lesson plans. To focus our attention on these relationships and linkages of genres, Bazerman (1994) suggested we consider genre systems and the way such a system frames each single use of a genre to carry out a set of intentions within systematic relations.

Russell (1997a, 1997b) further suggested that the genre systems be considered within larger activity systems. Activity systems consist of regularized organized arrangements that facilitate communal pursuit of objects (Leontiev, 1978). Following on Vygotsky's (1978, 1986) interest in tools and signs in mediating human activity, activity theory sees the ongoing culture of a group embodied in the artefacts that mediate the work of the group (Cole, 1996). Texts may be seen as such mediating artifacts (tools and signs that enable the coordinated work), and genres may be seen as means of providing regularity and orderliness to the ongoing communal processes of activity. Engestrom (1996) has also pointed to the importance of rules and the division of labor that mediate the individual's relationship with the community and with the communal object. Genres may also be understood as vehicles of regulation through their formation of expectations and of division of labor through the rights and responsibilities people in different social roles have to read and write in various genres.

Russell (1997a) points out that not only can one map out the work of text-mediated activity systems through the distribution and timing of genres within the activity group, one may also understand how work and meaning flows from one activity group to another through the flow of documents and the relations between genres in one activity system and another. Thus claims from articles that originally appeared within the activity system of biological research eventually find their way into the activity systems of classrooms either in the form of textbook knowledge or in the form of reprints of classic articles. Many of the studies on writing in the disciplines, professions, and across the curriculum have used genre and activity theory including Bawarshi (2000, 2001, 2003); Bazerman (1988, 1999); Berkenkotter and Huckin (1995); Blakeslee (2001); Casanave (1995, 2002); Dias, et al. (1999); Geisler (1994); Gunnarson (1997); Haas (1993, 1996); Macdonald (1994); McCarthy (1991); McCarthy and Gerring (1994); Myers (1990a); Prior (1998); Smart (1993, 1999, 2000, 2002); Van Nostrand (1997); and Winsor (1996, 2003). Collections of research essays using genre and activity theories include Bazerman and Paradis (1991); Freedman and Medway (1994 a, 1994b); Dias, et al. (1999); Coe, Lingard, and Teslenko (2002); Russell and Bazerman (1997); Bazerman and Russell (2003).

Two other related views of genre come out of the functional linguistic world. Within Structural functional Linguistics (see M. A. K. Halliday, 1985) genre is viewed as a "staged, goal-oriented social process" (Martin, Christie, & Rothery, 1987, p. 58). This view is elaborated in Hasan and Martin (1989) and Martin (1992); related views are elaborated in Cope and Kalantzis (1993) and Kress (1987). Within the applied linguistic field of English for specific purposes, attention has been given to the various rhetorical moves enacted within the sections of specific genres. The most well-known example of this analysis is Swales' "create a research space " model of the introductory section of a scientific research paper. According to this model an introduction establishes a research territory by showing the importance of the area and reviewing the literature; defines a niche for the current work by indicating a gap, question, or limitation of previous work; and occupies that niche by stating the goal of the current study (Swales, 1990; see also Bhatia, 1993).

Intertextuality

A genre system and activity theory system approach to texts also directs one towards a theory of intertextuality. For texts within systems rely on, refer to, incorporate, supersede, or otherwise relate to one another. The term intertextuality was first coined by Julia Kristeva (1980) in a work of literary theory *Desire in Language: A Semiotic Approach to Literature and Art,* where she suggests that any text is a mosaic of quotations. She finds the origin of her thinking in Volosinov's (1986) *Marxism and the Philosophy of Language* (originally published in 1929 and sometimes attributed to Mikhail Bakhtin). Volosinov argues that language exists only in individual utterances located in particular moments, histories, and relations; one cannot properly understand language apart from its instances of use, embedded within many surrounding utterances. Volosinov, furthermore, begins a technical analysis of how texts position themselves to each other through linguistic systems of direct and indirect quotations. That relation among texts is in large part organized by genre within activity systems. Fundamentally all the other genres and texts that previously occurred within the activity system are part of the intertextual context of any new text. The new text may explicitly or implicitly refer to those prior texts and their consequences. A proposal is constrained by the request it is responding to, plus it picks up topics, project specifics, and criteria to address from the request for proposals. The agreement to accept the proposal echoes materials from both previous documents, and so on until the work and project are completed. Moreover, within a genre one is expected or allowed to draw on or refer to texts of specific other genres from either the same activity system or other particular systems. Thus science textbooks rely on the research and handbook literature of the field, but cite them in different ways than other research articles. The textbooks codify, select, sequence on pedagogic principles, and explain in a unified way the aggregate of knowledge gained from the literature, where as research articles use the literature as resources to make the case for their new claims or competitors to be removed. For a fuller consideration of intertextuality in writing (see Porter, 1986; Selzer, 1993b; Bazerman, in press).

8

On-Going Concerns: The Place of Students in Disciplinary Discourses

What students attend to, work on, and learn in all educational settings very much depends on student attitudes, engagement, socialization, and sense of agency within the learning situations. This is particularly crucial in considering students' involvement within disciplinary material that may be at some distance from their everyday sense of the world and their lives. WAC particularly highlights these issues of student stance as writing puts students on the spot to communicate within situations where disciplinary knowledge is by definition a central resource and component. Thus, it is not surprising that questions of student position, stance, voice, and agency with academic and disciplinary discourses has generated controversy and discussion.

Student Orientation toward Disciplinary Assignments

Case studies have illuminated how students perceive and prepare for school-related tasks and activities, by allowing researchers to examine students' real-life struggles and successes. Prior (1998) presents one such account in *Writing/Disciplinarity: A Sociohistoric Account of Literate Activity in the Academy,* in which he traces the instructor's and students' responses to the major assignments and activities involved in a graduate seminar. He found that each of the students and the instructor viewed the tasks of the assignments differently, resulting in a range of different work pursued and different products handed in.

Studies of classroom writing indicate the teacher's pedagogical style, ideology, and objectives can strongly influence the students' writing (Casanave, 1995; Herrington, 1985, 1988; Prior, 1998). Since the instructor usually designs the course, selects course readings, sets assignments, and organizes class activities, this impact is not surprising. In Prior's example of the language research course, the instructor identified three major course and assignment objectives relating to curricular (occurring within a specific institutional context), professional (as part of a disciplinary discourse community), and developmental areas (as part of an intellectual process into which students are being assimilated). In order to contextualize the assignment of a literature review, the instructor told how in a previous class he had had to renegotiate the assignment based on one student's desire to include every study ever published on the topic rather than compile a more tailored, selective list. The instructor's request to submit "just a draft" of their research proposal took on a variety of meanings; however, most interpreted it to mean "rough draft" or an "easy assignment." Although their instructor's directives certainly influenced several of their decisions in the course, many students commented that personal interests, life experiences, and political or ethical issues were inextricably linked to the topics chosen for their research proposals. Some were more practical with their research topics allowing availability of research materials to direct their selections. "In short," Prior remarks, "students' research proposals and critiques were embedded in and infused with motives, contexts, and resources that extended well beyond the seminar" (Prior, 1998, p. 49).

Flower, et al. (1990) observed that variation among student texts was often not simply a reflection of their quality of work but rather of their understanding of the task at hand. Equally paramount was their finding that both teachers and students assumed task representations were the same when in fact each may have had different expectations for assignment objectives. Spivey (1988) also found that students' interpretations of assignments differed significantly from instructor's intentions, with perceptions strongly shaped by what they were actually rewarded for. Kirsch (1988) documents the substantial amount of work and dialogue that went into creating alignment between the instructor's intentions and the student's understanding of the task; interestingly through this dialog the student came to understand that the instructor was not being as directive in expectations as he had imagined, and that he as writer needed to take ownership of the assignment more confidently.

In *Genre Knowledge in Disciplinary Communication,* Berkenkotter and Huckin (1995) note the reluctance of American language arts and composition teachers to spend class time teaching the genre conventions of the disciplines. In the U.K. and Australia, however, the explicit instruction of genres in the classroom has been the source of intense disagreement, culminating with *The Place of Genre in Learning: A Current Debate* (Reid, 1987), a collection representing various positions on the subject. One contributor, Gunther Kress, remarked that the real issue regarding allowing students creativity with the conventions of genre was whether children's experimentation would actually be deemed successful or whether it would, perhaps as Flower et al. observed, be perceived as a submission of sub-par work (Kress, 1987). In *Language, Schooling, and Society* (1985), Christie argued "that a major cause of many primary and elementary school children's inability to learn written genres other than narrative is that teachers do not make explicit their tacit and seemingly unreflexive knowledge of classroom genres. Such knowledge constitutes the *hidden curriculum* of the language arts classroom" (p. 21). The existence of these overseas debates confirms the significance of the issue and raises the question whether students are being adequately prepared for the kinds of work expected of them in the disciplines.

Domination, Participation, and Agency

While WAC as both a theory and a practice has espoused the ideals of student empowerment through language and student entry into disciplinary discourses that were once mysterious if not closed to them, it is not without its critics. Within the broader field of composition, the battles rage over whether writing instruction as commonly carried out in the university is equipping students with linguistic tools or coercing them into accepting the dominant discourse. In WAC, difference is usually considered at the disciplinary level, with each discipline's linguistic and rhetorical practices respected and students encouraged to develop adaptability in writing in response to these disciplinary differences.

The field of composition has been forced, however, through rigorous public discussion and debate, to come to terms with issues of race, class, and gender as they relate to the writing process and to the discourse communities which house writing. WAC will continue to be challenged along these lines as well. Delpit (1993), in "The Politics of Teaching Literate Discourse," notes the dilemma instructors feel when teaching non-mainstream students to conform to mainstream standards. She wonders, "Does it not smack of racism or classism to demand that these students put aside the language of their homes and communities and adopt a discourse that is not only alien, but that has been instrumental in furthering their oppression?" (Delpit, 1993, p. 207). Delpit ultimately argues that dominant discourses such as academic discourse need not be oppressive to students of color, but the extent to which she respectfully addresses these concerns is evidence of the weight of these concerns. Villanueva (2001) also argues that disciplinary discourses are assimilationist, and that WAC instructors should become aware of the voices students bring with them from their cultures and the ways these voices are expressed within early drafts of their academic papers. Such an awareness will enable these voices to be translated into the academic world rather than suppressed and excluded. McCrary (2001) similarly comments that developmental writers—typically students from less privileged backgrounds—are less able to tap relevant reservoirs of knowledge when they are assigned academic texts. Further, he finds academic writing is valorized without justification. To counter this situation which further marginalizes non-mainstream students, he advocates use of texts reflecting womanist theology as a way to provide students with "an accessible discourse and hermeneutic that challenges and critiques oppressive rhetoric both inside and outside the academy" (McCrary, 2001, p. 549).

Halasek (1999) questions whether academic discourse offers students the rhetorical position they need to speak with authority to a reader/teacher. Halasek is interested in changing the academy to fit the students' language uses, not changing their language use to fit the academy. Halasek does not, however, call for an abolition of academic discourse from writing instruction; rather she wants to counter pedagogical approaches that emphasize conventions and form over that which is generative and critical.

LeCourt (1996) also seeks appropriate writing stances for students who do not find their voice within disciplinary discourses. The danger, to LeCourt and others who favor a critical pedagogy, is that the students' voices will be silenced as they are forced to submit to the prevailing discourse conventions and to reproduce the "dominant ideologies" which the discourse supports. This silencing is particularly troubling, as LeCourt details, when it involves "cultural, socio-economic, and gender differences as well as alternative literacies and other ways of knowing" (p. 396). LeCourt suggests a two-pronged approach to the problem of addressing these issues in a WAC program. First, "disciplinary writing can—and perhaps should—be examined by both disciplinary practitioners as well as students in order to reveal exclusions and enclosures of discourse to see how and why they developed and to question their necessity in any particular case" (LeCourt, 1996, p. 396). This sort of critical thinking about disciplinary discourse can, according to LeCourt, allow students to "(1) recognize the continual conflicts currently being played out within the discourse, (2) examine the influence of wider social discourses on their construction, and (3) interrogate how a discourse's constitution is both productive and silencing" (LeCourt, 1996, p. 397). Second, LeCourt suggests a renewed emphasis on expressivist writing, especially in writing to learn, as "a way for the personal and disciplinary to interact in a dialectical fashion rather than one in which one voice must be silenced for the other to speak" (LeCourt, 1996, p. 400). For an earlier, similar critique, see Mahala (1991).

Elbow (1998) argues the way to develop students' intellectual stance necessary for producing academic discourse is through doing non-academic writing. This frees students to develop their thoughts without the burden of following conventional surface features of academic writing. He believes that the deep structure of academic discourse is no different from the deep structure of good nonacademic discourse. Only the surface features or mannerisms of academic discourse differ, and students can best learn the intellectual stance without having to worry about surface mannerisms. In fact, he believes that students can be seduced by the surface dimensions, adherence to which may hide the failure of students to "engage fully in the intellectual task" (Elbow, 1998, p. 162).

Zamel (1998) also believes that direct instruction in academic writing too often is "reduced to identifying the language, conventions, and generic forms that supposedly represent the various disciplines" (Zamel, 1998, p. 187) rather than the serious underlying intellectual work. Moreover, the valorization of objectifying conventions of other disciplines may come at the expense of the humanistic traditions of personal engagement and accepts a hierarchical subordination to the standards and interests of other disciplines.

Bazerman (1992, 2002) argues that the social power of various disciplinary languages is the very reason that students should become conversant with these languages. Students gain from the ability to carry out their own perceptions and interests within those powerful worlds held together by specialized languages or learn to contend effectively against their effects. Even more, learning to participate in disciplinary discourses goes beyond learning conventional forms to learning to use the disciplinary tools effectively to think, investigate, and formulate arguments. Although disciplinary languages may follow conventions, those conventions arose out of histories of contention and argument, and often carry serious intellectual weight. The particular modes of investigation and argument are the products of serious attempts to understand and find meaning in the world, and then to act for human purposes in relation to the world. Attempting to remove ourselves from particular forms of entanglement in the world (i.e., creating various forms of "objectivity") has been found to be useful in some of those inquiries just as, in other kinds of inquiry, finding various ways to explore, expand, and reformulate our subjectivities has been useful. Humanistic inquiries stand side by side with social scientific, scientific, and other professional inquiries, but we should not be in a position of prejudging for our students which will be most useful and valuable for them.

While challenging students' previous perceptions, experiences, and commitments, disciplinary modes of thought and action provide opportunities for expansion of identities and strengthening new voices that are effective in powerful communities. To suggest that students not pursue and engage new worlds because of previous commitments suggests that some groups of people should not have access to or influence to shape influential knowledge communities that will impact their lives. Professions and disciplines exert great force in contemporary society, and that force has dangerous and oppressive potentials. These disciplines and professions, nonetheless, are the construction of people's commitments to do good work in the world, expand knowledge, and carry out significant tasks to the best of our human abilities. Intelligent choice making, participation, and attempts to transform contemporary practice need critical acumen, but careful criticism and tools to redirect disciplines only come through detailed engagement with them. Only by engaging with, learning to use, and effectively exercising those powers can we make them part of a world we want to live in. Only by making these worlds accessible to our students can we provide them means to live within them and exercise the powerful forms of inquiry that shape our contemporary forms of life.

Part III. Practical Guidelines

9

New Programmatic Directions

As experience, research, and theory relevant to WAC have developed so have programmatic issues and initiatives. New ways of organizing student writing experiences across the curriculum have grown, as have ways of reaching more students, and ways of monitoring the success of students and of programs. One of the best general sources to look for new programmatic developments in WAC is the collection *WAC for the New Millennium* (McLeod, et al., 2001). A number of the programmatic developments in WAC have to do with coordinating with other curricular offerings (writing intensive courses) and other campus services (writing centers and peer tutors). Serving the needs of second language students within a WAC Program has also become a matter of programmatic concern. Other efforts have been aimed at changing the character of student experiences, by organizing students into self-support groups (Interdisciplinary Learning Communities) and by engaging students in disciplinary-based hands-on learning experiences using writing (service learning). Two other programmatic initiatives have been aimed at enhancing writing opportunities through electronic communication (Electronic Communication Across the Curriculum) and developing assessment tools appropriate for the evaluation of student writing in disciplinary contexts and the evaluation of WAC Programs.

Coordinating with Other Campus Resources

Writing Intensive Courses

Writing intensive courses are an institutional method of putting greater stress on student writing throughout a greater range of courses and of providing support for student writing in those courses. Typically a number of general education and/or more advanced courses in the major are designated writing intensive, writing enhanced, or writing in the major. These courses, then, are required to assign at least a certain amount of writing and count that writing as a significant component of the grade. Typically students must then complete a certain number of those courses in order to graduate.

Farris and Smith (1992) in their article, "Writing Intensive Courses: Tools for Curricular Change," identify some general characteristics of writing intensive courses.

1. Small (or at least limited) class size

2. Taught by faculty instead of TA's

3. Page and/or word count requirements for each course

4. Revision requirements

5. Writing makes up a certain varying percentage of the final grade

6. Some guidelines regarding types of assignments (i.e. not just a "term paper" at the end of the course)

7. Evaluation guidelines given to instructors

8. WI workshops, WAC consultation and/or writing center tutoring

According to Farris and Smith, the most common feature is a page or word count requirement. Townsend (2001), however, points out within that general framework, that details of WI courses are highly local due to their need to be institutionally specific.

The WI course approach and WAC share a commitment to spreading the responsibility for writing instruction "across the curriculum" and many WI programs also are similar to WAC programs in their promotion of writing-to-learn assignments within courses. The WI course approach nonetheless can be criticized for ghettoizing writing within specific designated courses rather than integrating writing into all courses. Students in schools with WI programs sometimes complain when writing is assigned in non-WI courses and WI courses are often doled out to junior faculty. Also legislated writing requirements in non-writing courses can become increasingly nominal and periph-

eral to the course. Requirements may be ignored unless the requirement is monitored. The key to a successful WI requirement that is
viewed positively by faculty and students is continuous support for
the disciplinary instructors incorporating writing into their courses in
ways that are meaningful for the learning goals of that course.

Writing Centers

Writing centers can have a variety of forms, functions and missions
within a university. There are as many organizational "types" of writing centers as there are colleges and universities that put them into
place. But almost all deliver one-on-one tutorial support for students
in their writing for all courses and almost all place emphasis on fundamental issues of learning to write rather than simply providing a
proofreading or correction service.

   Writing centers and WAC grew up together due to open admissions, changing university population demographics, a new emphasis on job skills, and increased focus on institutional accountability.
These changes in the university environment coupled with the "writing crisis" led to the development of both WAC programs and writing
centers. Like WAC, writing centers tend to reject a one-size-fits-all
writing instruction approach and instead strives to explore disciplinary
differences in writing and differing faculty expectations within those
disciplines (Mullin 2001). See also Barnett & Blumner (1999).

   Some schools do not have formal WAC programs, per se, but the
university writing center serves writing in all courses and implements
writing across the curriculum activities. Alternatively, schools establish
a WAC program and as faculty assign more and varied writing, the
need for a writing center becomes apparent in order to assist students
with these assignments. In some WAC programs, the WC acts as a hub
within the university community, offering services to both students
and faculty. Some WC's go beyond this and offer outreach services to
the larger community's citizens and institutions.

   In a recent book, *Demythologizing Language Differences in the
Academy: Establishing Discipline-Based Writing Programs,* Mark Waldo
(2004) argues that Writing Centers are the best site for the development of WAC programs. Because writing centers can be institutionally
separate from any department they can take the languages, projects,
and forms of creativity of participating disciplines seriously on their
own terms, apart from the language beliefs and commitments of the

department which would house the writing program. He also provides many detailed suggestions about developing and running such a center, along with the training of tutors who would carry out an inquiry-based approach that attends to linguistic differences of departments.

Peer Tutors and Writing Fellows

In the early days of WAC, peer tutors were seen as ancillary, part of a support service for students confined to the WC on campus. Curriculum-based peer tutor programs have their roots in the Brown University Writing Fellows Program, though Harriett Sheridan is credited with first linking peer tutors with WAC programs at Carleton College and later helping Tori Haring-Smith in the establishment of a similar program at Brown. The role of peer tutors has grown in importance over the past decade, though, and a new brand of tutor has evolved: the curriculum-based peer tutor. Mullin (2001) explains that these tutors work within a program of "tutor-linked courses" (189). Writing tutors, sometimes referred to as "writing fellows," are assigned to undergraduate courses and work with the students in those courses on writing assignments. Soven states, "In the curriculum-based model, peer tutors are written into the plan of instruction. They are part of the course, which gives them a distinctly different role than that of the writing center tutor" (Soven 2001, p.204). These tutors generally assist students by reading drafts and conferencing, however some tutors provide in-class tutoring, conduct discussions or give classroom presentations.

Curriculum-based peer tutors act as a practical means of achieving WAC goals by providing concrete assistance to instructors (Song & Richter 1997). Debate is ongoing regarding the qualifications of tutors in a curriculum-based peer tutor program. Many argue that tutors should be majoring in the discipline where the course is located so that they may provide a more "expert" reading of the papers students write. Others argue for the "generalist" tutor whose expertise lies in writing and the writing process, leaving the content of papers to the judgment of the individual professors. Whether from the major or not, tutors usually get specialized training and support in providing writing assistance, either through an academic course or series of required workshops.

English as a Second Language in a WAC Context

The changing demographics of many universities combined with an increasing understanding of the advanced academic needs of students from whom English is a second language have led more systematic concern for how those students can be supported in a WAC environment. The students needing additional, directed support are not only foreign students or recent immigrants (traditional ESL students), they include students who may have been in the country for a number of years, long enough to gain fluency, but have not gained the skills of advanced academic literacy. They may even be born and educated in the U.S. but lack expertise in either their family's original language or English. Such educated in the U.S. ESL students are sometimes called Generation 1.5 (Harklau, Losey, & Siegal 1999). Even when such students have gained fluency, they may have cultural differences that may stand in the way of understanding the expectations of writing in their various courses (Johns 1991) and may lead them to prefer courses and majors with fewer language demands and fewer culture specific presumptions. While students with more limited English Language proficiency may be provided focused ESL instruction, all will at some point be likely to enter into the mainstream curriculum, not only in English but in courses throughout the curriculum. Johns (2001, pp. 141–164) provides a good overview of ESL issues confronting WAC programs.

When ESL students turn up in regular English language courses (and even more when they turn up in disciplinary classes which have substantial writing requirements) their patterned errors, transitional forms of language, unidiomatic expressions and different assumptions about desired academic performances may cause their writing to be stigmatized as showing lack of academic talent (Zamel 1995). Students struggling with the forms and expectations of the language, who do not have deeply habituated patterns of correct usage, need time and opportunities to revise in order to bring their sentences to standard form. Further their struggles with language take attention away from the intellectual tasks of any piece of writing, or if students focus on the intellectual challenge, they divert attention from formal correctness. Because of the need for conscious revision to bring the language to standard form, errors are particularly likely to turn up in timed writing, as on exams; when assignments require a higher level of complexity and cognitive challenge; and alternatively when students feel that their writing will not be held to formal standards (Leki 2004). Sensitizing writing teachers and instructors of writing intensive disciplinary courses to the kinds of struggles ESL students have with the language can help them respond more appropriately and usefully to student productions.

But the difficulties ESL students may have with WAC go beyond formal correctness. Because of cultural patterns of self-presentation and argument, as well as cultural differences in schooling and school writing, students may produce inappropriate or ineffective work even if the work is formally correct. Cultural differences are likely to turn up quickly on the issue of plagiarism. Some cultures, for example, expect accomplished writes to incorporate phrases of the classic literature without comment. And in some educational systems one is expected to show that one has learned the material by repeating assigned readings verbatim on exams, rather than rephrasing to show your understanding. Finally, ESL students, because of more limited vocabulary are more likely to repeat well-phrased originals rather than to seek alternatives (Leki 2004).

The field of Contrastive Rhetoric helps explain some of the differences in stance, argument, explicitness, and text organization that students from other cultures and trained in other languages might take and also provides teachers means to explain to their students the alternative expectations of their own assignments. (Connor and Kaplan 1987; Connor 1996; Purves 1988; Li 1996). Even more deeply, differences in students expectations of education may lead them to dissatisfaction and alienation form the education offered from their classes and may create difficulties in finding productive ways to respond to assignments (Casanave 1992). The more fully and explicitly the assumptions of education can be presented and the expectations and purposes of assignments can be made explicit, the more likely the ESL student can find ways of meaningfully participating and producing writing that speaks to the purposes and forms of the course. (Casanave 1995). Much of the work of ESP discussed in a previous chapter is aimed at making explicit the forms and purposes of writing in university classrooms. One particularly useful collection exploring the implications of a Genre approach to ESP is Johns 2002, *Genre in the Classroom*. Among other things the book has a chapter on teaching the literature review by Swales & Lindemann. Also useful are textbooks written from an ESP perspective such as Huckin & Olson 1991; Swales and Feak 2000.

Casanave (2002) in the book *Writing Games* considers the complex struggles ESL writers undergo in order to survive their writing assignments. Through an extensive examination of the case study literature on undergraduate, graduate, and professorial academic writing to which she adds many of her own case studies, she comes to see students developing strategies to address local, situated writing games in their classes. Learning the rules and conventions of the game are only part of the story as one also must want to play, develop a strategy and respond to the complex contingencies of the unfolding situation with appropriate tactical decisions. Through the case studies focusing on literacy practices she gives a strong sense from the students' perspective of what it takes to succeed in academic writing in different disciplines. She also provides some good general strategies that students can adopt.

Enriching Student Experiences

Interdisciplinary Learning Communities

Learning Communities serve to forge relations between students who are engaged in similar studies so that they can learn collaboratively, provide mutual support, and increase each other's engagement in the learning process. According to Zawacki and Williams (2001), learning communities are "curriculum change initiatives that link, cluster or integrate two or more courses during a given term, often around an interdisciplinary theme, and involve a common cohort of students" (109). While Learning Communities vary in their organization depending on the institution, they share the goals of "fostering greater academic coherence and more explicit intellectual connections among students, between students and their faculty, and among disciplines" (109).

Three of the most common variations of Learning Communities are:

1. Sections of a first year composition course are linked to a large disciplinary lecture course

2. Fully linked sections of two or more courses with overlapping syllabi and reading/writing assignments

3. Fully linked sections of courses with some sort of service learning component

Some plans for Learning Communities go so far as to house students with similar schedules together in the dorms and to provide some courses and support services in the dorms themselves.

Both WAC and Learning Communities or linked courses see writing as a vehicle or tool for reflective and critical development in students. Zawacki and Williams view Learning Communities as an expansion of the ideas behind WAC as they encourage genuine interdisciplinary collaboration and cooperation. They state that "WAC may be most fully realized within the learning communities movement, which shares its values of inclusiveness, conversation, and collaboration, and the belief that writing should be a central mode of learning in a learning-centered pedagogy" (137).

Service Learning

Service learning brings students out of the classroom to provide useful service for the community. While engaged in this service, students study the meaningful application of their disciplinary learning to serious community needs (Zlotkowski 1998). Often writing is incorporated in service learning courses as a means of identifying disciplinary knowledge useful for the service tasks, to report back on the service experiences and their disciplinary implications, and to carry out the actual service work (Jolliffe 2001).

WAC and service learning developed during roughly the same time period out of similar motives, but they have generally remained separate entities, both nationally and within individual institutions. Because of their common interest in making learning more meaningful, in supporting writing within motivated practice, and providing students the technical tools for valued accomplishments, some institutional convergence has occurred between service learning and first year composition programs. In 1998, the 4 C's launched an effort to bring service learning and composition together led by Thomas Deans who went on to author "Writing Partnerships: Service Learning in Composition" (2000), a description of composition programs incorporating a community service component.

According to Deans, WAC and service learning have much in common. He lists the following nine links:

1. Pedagogy that aims for more effective student learning

2. Departs from "traditional teaching and learning in college courses"; curricular innovation is valued

3. Have potential for cross-disciplinarity

4. Can promote re-visioning within disciplines

5. Often touted by administrators, students and parents

6. Often devalued by "old school academics"

7. Can be "perceived to take time away from content and lower standards"

8. Have found support in secondary education circles

9. Have developed along a cautious and careful path due to the conservative nature of higher education

Much potential exists in the linking of WAC with service learning programs because they both have writing at their center. Jolliffe sees the greatest potential in WAC's ability to collaborate with service learning programs in the area of genre. He suggests that WAC could help inform genre choices within service learning courses.

Electronic Communication Across the Curriculum

The WAC movement from the very beginning implied Reading Across the Curriculum because all disciplinary writing relies on and refers to the prior texts of the field. It soon easily expanded to encompass other communication forms, casting them as a set of interrelated activities fundamental to academic success. "While continuing to envision writing as central to the academic enterprise," explain Reiss, Selfe, and Young (1998, p. xvii), "such CAC [communication across the curriculum] programs emphasize speaking, visual communication, reading, critical thinking, advocacy, social negotiation, and problem solving across the curriculum." At the same time, the advent of the personal computer (PC) provided educators with relatively affordable word-processing systems, which quickly made their way into the writing classroom. Over time, networking hardware and software further enhanced the computer environment by enabling students to share their work, collaborate, and engage in peer review with students at a distance, both synchronously (e.g., chatrooms) and asynchronously (e.g., email, newsgroups, World Wide Web). So it was this 1980s emergence of the computer-supported writing environment, combined with the communication across the curriculum (CAC) movement, itself an outgrowth of WAC, that formed the foundation of what Reiss, Selfe, and Young (1998) have recently called "electronic communication across the curriculum," or ECAC: a movement that "recognizes that e-mail, synchronous and asynchronous conferencing, multimedia, and the World Wide Web offer new modes of communication to construct and enhance learning within and across the disciplines" (p. 306).

The introduction of computers into the composition classroom generally encouraged process-oriented pedagogies by incorporating revision operations like cut-and-paste into word processing functionality. Nonetheless, some educators initially used computers as automated grammar and spelling monitors, reinforcing a pedagogy of mechanical error correction and automated drill instruction (Reiss, Self, & Young, 1998, p. xii; Hawisher et al., 1996, pp. 17–63). In 1980, Robert Taylor offered a classification scheme that cast the various instructional software available to educators in the functional light of tutorials, style tools, and programming environments; soon thereafter, Helen Schwartz (1982) identified simulation as another dimension of computer technology relevant to education. The writing-as-inquiry and writing-as-process movements had expanded teachers' conceptions of computers beyond that of mechanical tutorial devices for ensuring "correctness" in English language usage. Process-oriented articles in *CCC*, such as "Computerized Word-Processing as an Aid to Revision" (Bean, 1983) and "The Computer as Stylus and Audience," (Daiute, 1983) began to appear.

Kenneth Bruffee's (1984) review essay, "Collaborative Learning and the 'Conversation of Mankind,'" combined with Fred Kemp's (1987) scheme, which reorganized instructional software into current-traditional, expressive, cognitive, and social categories, to open up a different approach to the use of electronic tools in the teaching of writing based on the interpersonal or networked function of computer technology, by way of email and bulletin boards (Hawisher, 1994). Sometime during this decade, "computer-aided" came to mean "networked" or "wired" in the context of the composition classroom. The realization that computer technology could sponsor a socially interactive and collaborative environment, virtually freed from the constraints of geographic proximity, within which students could come to more authentic meanings through social negotiation flourished within the field (Duin & Hansen, 1994). The work of Clifford Geertz, Mikhail Bakhtin, Thomas Kuhn, and Richard Rorty now figured prominently in discussions of electronic communities of learning, largely by way of Bruffee. The advent of the World Wide Web and its accessible programming language, Hypertext Markup Language (HTML), dramatically fueled the nascent ECAC movement by offering students concrete and creative fora for electronic participation beyond the emerging modes of email, newsgroups, and bulletin boards. Early studies were patently optimistic: Schrum (1988) characterized the new interaction among networked students as purposeful and motivating, a point shared by Mageau (1990). In their study of an electronic discussion list set up to aid students' understandings of class readings, Cooper and Selfe (1990) found that students resisted what they perceives as academic roles and instead inhabited more personal roles as they engaged and discussed the texts, thereby becoming more active and more responsible for their understanding. The element of anonymity and lack of face-to-face interaction eliminated the potential for age, gender, race, or social status discrimination, according to Cooper and Selfe, and enabled the sharing of ideas rather than the confronting of personalities to become the centerpeice of the electronic classroom. In "They Became What They Beheld," Stuart Moulthrop and Nancy Kaplan (1994) explore the value of hypertextuality in literature, characterizing the new medium as an "evolutionary outgrowth of late-modern textuality" (p. 221). Through its open-endedness, hyptertextuality encourages new ways of affiliating and interacting with the text, often sponsoring renewed interest and active student participation, as well as new ways of conceptualizing reader-writer relationships as well as the concept of authorship.

By the 1990s, however, many teachers, practitioners, and scholars were turning a critical eye toward this latest revolution in educational technology. In "The Effect of Hypertext on Processes of Reading and Writing," Davida Charney (1994) cautions that hypertextuality may actually impede learning owing to its disruptive process and loose structure, which places the burden of organization upon the reader.

Also critical is Paul LeBlanc (1994) who laments the fundamental inequity in quality of and access to computer technology across school districts. While some schools embody the vision of computer-enhanced literacy learning by equipping students with high-performance computers connected through high-speed networks and supported by trained technical staffs, the majority of schools LeBlanc visited offered dilapidated computer environments, often the result of ill-preparedness on the part of administration. The "dazzling simulation and critical skills programs" available in the expensive labs, combined with the successful social interaction over high-speed networks, stood in sharp and painful contrast to the more common and less-expensive classroom scenarios in which several children were required to share a single computer running drill-and-practice routines and meager word processing capabilities (p. 25). In many cases, schools simply did not budget for network technology, and in at least one case, notes LeBlanc (1994, p. 25), two new Apple computers sat under dustcovers in the back of a classroom because the administrator did not budget for software or peripherals. One of the most palpable benefits of ECAC, as Betsy Bowen (1994, p. 118) notes, has been the introduction of an authentic audience, in the form of students' virtual peers, thereby decreasing the commonly criticized artificiality of the composition classroom. But for LeBlanc and others like him, the question becomes: For whom?

In recent years, the ECAC movement has begun to fulfill its vision by expanding beyond the walls of the composition classroom. According to Muriel Harris (1998), ECAC has played a large role in transforming traditional writing centers into online writing labs (OWL) but in ways that we might not expect. Initially, writing centers frequently offered email tutoring as a progressive way to meet student needs, and more recently centers have experimented with online Multi-user dimension, Object Oriented environments (MOO) as a means by which to meet and exchange rough drafts of papers with students in a flexible and constructive setting. Yet, according to Harris, neither email nor MOOs successfully gained student participation. Owing to its asynchronous interaction, email lacked real-time interaction and results, two hot commodities on college campus; students prefer walking into a physical writing center and receiving immediate feedback on a first-come, first-served basis. Although MOOs offer a synchronous or real-time environment, current technological limitations in

terms of bandwidth and processor speed often limit the sharable data
to text-based interactions. As a result, much of the visual and auditory
interaction requisite for successful student-tutor sessions is lost or, even
with state-of-the-art technology, disruptive. Ironically, one of the most
successful ways in which computer technology has enhanced the writing center is not through distance education but by complementing
the traditional, face-to-face interactions between students and tutors.
With the aid of the World Wide Web, online search engines, online library catalogs, and CD-ROM-based periodical indexes, tutors are able
to assist writers more fully throughout the writing process, especially
common prewriting activities. Tutors are able to assist writers in what
Irene Clark calls "information literacy" skills, or the "ability to access,
retrieve, evaluate, and integrate information from a variety of electron-
ically generated resources" (qtd. in Harris, 1998, p. 5). Face-to-face,
local interactions aside, the ECAC movement has also been successful
in another area: providing students, teachers, administrators, and professionals around the world with up-to-date writing handouts by way
of the World Wide Web. According to Harris (1998), this is one of the
most popular aspects of many online writing centers.

10

Assessment in Writing Across the Curriculum

The development of WAC programs raised two kinds of assessment questions—concerning assessing students' work and assessing the success of programs.

First, student writing needed to be assessed in a new context. WAC in its very principles challenged the traditional assessment based on general skills displayed in undifferentiated testing situations. WAC highlighted that there were many different forms of writing that varied from discipline to discipline, and what counted as good writing for a literature class would not pass muster in a physics lab, and vice-versa. Moreover, WAC points out how closely forms of writing are tied to the knowledge and activities mobilized in any writing task. Finally, WAC points to the active construction of learning and knowledge by the student in the course of writing, so that it is not appropriate to measure writing simply against a fixed standard.

Second, assessments of WAC programs were even more problematic than the known difficulties of assessing writing programs. The heterogeneity of WAC programs, the range of faculty involved, and the multiple desired outcomes of student performance made the display and measure of a program's accomplishments and shortcomings a complex and uncertain matter.

Assessment of Student Writing.

This section attempts to answer the following questions: How is student writing assessed in disciplinary classrooms? What is expected of student writing in writing across the curriculum classes, and how is this communicated to students? How is writing evaluated when writing is assigned as a learning tool (i.e., journals)?

Before looking at these questions, some definitions are needed. Among compositionists and writing researchers, there are several ways in which reaction to student writing is taken up. Some research and scholarship is focused on *response* to student writing; that is, how teachers, tutors, and peers respond, either verbally or in writing, to texts written by students. Another area of research considers the *evaluation* of student writing, including how writing performance influences decisions of student placement in educational settings. A third area looks at *assessment* of student writing; that is, the methods by which student writing is assessed, as well as the criterion, standards, or measures involved in the assessment. These areas are, of course, closely related, and by considering what scholars and researchers have to say about the response, assessment, and evaluation of student writing across the curriculum and in the disciplines, we can come to a better understanding of what it means to teach from a WAC/WID approach.

Writing is studied increasingly as a situated activity, and both the activity itself and the resulting texts produced by writers—whether students or professionals—are widely recognized as both embedded in and constructed by the social environment in which the writing operates (Bazerman & Paradis, 1994). But more than simply a way of saying that texts and writers are unique, a view of writing as a situated activity permits and requires a deeper and careful study of texts in context. One component of such study considers not the uniqueness of texts and writers but the ways in which they are conventional; that is, the ways in which texts and writers observe conventions operating within—perhaps even defining—the context of the text's production. Two "stories" emerge: in one story, the writer follows conventions in order to place his or her text within a network of other texts, activities, and participants. But the other story, equally important in understanding writing's situatedness, is that the writer contributes to the ongoing construction of conventions, not simply by enforcing the conventions through use, but by confirming and disconfirming the effectiveness, relevance, and appropriateness of the conventions in the face of changing needs, interests, goals, and circumstances.

In student writing, particularly student writing in disciplinary classrooms, the examination of writing and texts contains at least two distinct contexts: the context of the classroom and the context of the discipline. In order to understand, then, assessment of student writing across the curriculum and in the disciplines, it is necessary to consider how student writing is seen as a product of the classroom environment and as a product of the discipline. It stands to reason that, when writing is viewed as a product of the classroom, there will be a more consistent pattern of expectations and evaluations between teachers and across disciplines. Teachers, regardless of discipline, will tend to share a similar set of expectations and evaluations of student writing when considering that writing as a product of the classroom environment. Some of these expectations include such factors as compliance with specific instructions (i.e., page length, due dates, format), relevance to course material (i.e., choosing topics appropriate to the course), and use of standard written English. In addition, when texts are considered as a product of the classroom, teachers are likely to evaluate texts from the basis of what they indicate about the student's level of knowledge, as an indication of what the student has learned. This last expectation illustrates how teachers reading student writing is itself a product of the environment: teachers are less likely to assume knowledge of facts or information not explicitly included in a text written by student writers than in a text written by a professional writer.

In other words, the enterprise of learning operating in the classroom is fairly consistent and stable across teachers and disciplines, which leads to a fairly consistent and stable view of writing as a product of the classroom. Obviously, this view of writing as an aspect of learning will be influenced by individual teachers' views of teaching and learning, but in general, the principles governing how student writing is perceived will be limited to those dealing with learning. In addition, the variations among teachers in regards to views of writing as a product of the classroom is likely to be independent of their disciplinary affiliation; that is, teachers from different disciplines are likely to share similar views of writing as an expression of learning (Bean, 1996; Fulwiler, 1987b).

However, when student writing is considered as the product of a particular disciplinary environment, expectations of student writing, and the subsequent response, assessment, and evaluation, are more varied across disciplines, and there is a higher degree of consistency among teachers within a given discipline (VanSledright & Frankes, 1998). Teachers within a discipline are likely to expect similar things from student writing, and those expectations seem to be influenced more by the unique qualities or features of the discipline itself than by more personal elements such as taste or opinion. Even when dealing with freshmen writers, Schwegler and Shamoon (1991) found that sociology teachers expected students to use lines of reasoning and support unique to sociology. When reading student papers, the teachers studied rejected even those lines of reasoning and support drawn from related fields, such as anthropology and psychology. While there seemed to be more tolerance for "undisciplined" introductions, most participants in the study expected student papers to adhere to disciplinary constraints and conventions. The study suggests that teachers are particularly concerned with textual macrostructure, the gist and lines of reasoning employed in the paper.

In order to articulate disciplinary standards as well as to develop pedagogy and support of writing within the discipline, a group at North Carolina State University has been fostering discussions within each department participating in the WAC program. These discussions within each department, though facilitated by writing specialists, are driven by the disciplinary faculty. The discussions, however, center on student learning and student performance, and are carried forward in the context of concrete data about student accomplishment. The discussions address three questions:

(1) What are the outcomes—skills, knowledge, and other attributes—that graduates of the program should attain? (2) To what extent is the program enabling its graduates to attain the outcomes? And (3) How can the faculty use what they learn from program assessment to improve their programs so as to better enable graduates to attain the outcomes?

The set of questions moves issues of assessment of student performance directly to issues of program design and assessment and then to program improvement. (Carter, 2002; Carter, Anson, & Miller, forthcoming; Anson, Carter, Dannels, & Rust, forthcoming).

WAC Program Assessment and Evaluation

As WAC programs have moved from the first stage (development and first years of implementation) into the second stage (program maturity) (McLeod, 1989), the need and the desire to determine what these programs are accomplishing has given life to an entire literature of WAC assessment and evaluation. Within education, assessment and evaluation of programs are a common and expected parts of administration. Michael Williamson defines assessment as "gathering information useful to describe the operations of a program or curriculum" and evaluation as "ascribing merit based on the information gathered in an assessment (1997, p. 239). The methods, motives, subjects, and audiences of the assessment and evaluation of WAC programs are as varied and difficult to define as the programs themselves. Because, as Toby Fulwiler points out, "the local conditions that gave rise to WAC programs were always quite specific," (Fulwiler & Young, 1997, p. 1), the assessing and evaluating of those programs is largely dependent upon the needs and desires of the participants in those local programs.

Fulwiler (1988) outlined seven specific challenges to WAC assessment (pp. 62–64):

- WAC means different things on different campuses.

- The exigencies of running successful programs leave little funds, provide little data, and create little administrative motivation for in-depth evaluation.

- WAC programs evolve and mutate rapidly.

- WAC is carried out under different institutional arrangements on different campuses.

- Quick and dirty measures tell little.

- WAC programs are amorphous and open-ended.

- Successful WAC programs run deep into the center of the curriculum.

Consequently, much of the earlier assessment literature came in the form of accounts of program assessments and evaluations conducted—earlier accounts were largely anecdotal (see Fulwiler, 1984). Later studies of programs, however, are more methodical, often empirical (see Walvoord, et al., 1997). Since the mid-1990s, the move to theorize and analyze WAC program assessment has created another wave of literature.

In 1997, Kathleen Blake Yancey and Brian Huot edited a volume, *Assessing Writing Across the Curriculum: Diverse Approaches and Prac-*

tices, which brought together the expert voices in the field of WAC to discuss how program assessment had developed and how it might best be implemented by interested parties. Yancey and Huot lay out in the first chapter the purposes of assessment: 1) to see what the program is doing well; 2) to learn how the program can improve; and 3) to demonstrate to others why the program should continue or should be funded (p. 7). They then lay out the assumptions which guide the work in WAC assessment, which are that, first, WAC program assessment focuses on "the big picture"; second, it relies on guiding questions just as research does; third, it begins with "an explicit understanding about the nature of writing" (p. 7); fourth, it relies on diverse and often multiple methods; and fifth, it focuses on that point of interaction between teaching and learning with the goal of enhancing that interaction (pp. 8–11).

Looking at the big picture involves, by necessity, a narrowing of questions to be answered by any assessment. Kinkead (1997) approaches the design of an assessment process as "an opportunity to learn" (p. 39) and lays out a series of questions in a matrix divided by the categories of stakeholders (students, faculty, administrators):

- Who is assessed?

- What is assessed?

- Where is the locus of evaluation?

- Who is the audience of the assessment?

- Why is the assessment important or significant?

- How is the assessment to be conducted?

- When does the assessment occur?

Morgan (1997) suggests a business model for WAC assessment, likening it to the management principle of "total quality management" (TQM). According to Morgan, in TQM, the questions for assessment should ideally be determined at the point of program creation by setting measurable goals. The steps for assessment then become 1) set goals; 2) establish goal-achievement activities; and 3) create measures (p. 148). The questions arise naturally from the goals that have been set.

Selfe (1997) presents what she calls a "contextual model for evaluating WAC programs" (p. 51). This contextual model is essentially a social constructivist approach that requires assessors to move away from a positivistic view and instead view each program as socioculturally situated with the participants themselves constructing the program. Using this model, Selfe lays out not a series of questions–because they will be determined by the participants and their locally determined needs–but rather a series of steps:

- Collect benchmark information.

- Collect student and parent stories and histories regarding writing.

- Collect faculty stories and histories regarding writing and writing programs.

- Collect administrators' stories and histories regarding writing programs.

- Collect program artifacts.

- Conduct observations of WAC in action.

- Collect student performance artifacts (not limited to papers, but drafts, notes, etc.).

- Interview students and faculty.

A wide range of instruments for assessment and evaluation are mentioned in the literature. The most common are surveys and questionnaires given to faculty and to students. The surveys may be administered after a WAC faculty workshop, after a WAC-oriented course, after a program has been in place for a measure of time, or when an assessment is called for by an administration or accrediting organization. Other more qualitative instruments include interviews, again with faculty and students, observations in classrooms or writing centers, and examination of portfolios of student writing. According to Huot, the more conventional writing assessment procedures and instruments (i.e., the timed writing exam evaluated by trained readers, gauged for interrater reliability) present major difficulties when applied to WAC programs because the writing evaluated comes from a range of disciplines, each with their unique rhetorical features (1997, p. 70). What would be considered "good writing" in a chemistry course might be "atrocious" in an English literature course, hence the challenge of a generic evaluation of student writing.

Fulwiler (1988) points out that the goals of the program drive assessment. Only by understanding program goals can measurable factors be isolated and studied. He outlines five goals and presents possible measures for each (pp. 65–72):

- Building a Community of Scholars
    - Survey of who is participating in WAC workshops
    - Evaluations from participants after workshops
    - Follow-up surveys
- Pedagogy
    - Post-workshop evaluations
    - Survey or interviews that ask, "Do you notice a difference in your teaching?"
    - Comparison of syllabi before and after workshops
    - Student evaluations
- Improving Student Learning
    - Student interviews
    - Statistical studies of student performance before and after WAC program
- Improving Student Writing (the most common and most challenging goal to measure)
    - "Writing Apprehension Test" (see Daly & Miller, 1975)
    - Evaluation of student writing over the span of one course
    - Longitudinal, qualitative studies
- Improving Faculty Writing
    - Faculty interviews
    - Tracking of faculty articles, books, and presentations that involve WAC participation

Most assessment literature emphasizes that the outcomes of assessment can stretch well beyond the need to gain or maintain funding; the assessment process can, in itself, build bridges between program administrators and faculty working within the WAC program. Walvoord (1997) points out that faculty can play a variety of roles within the assessment process, ideally working as program creators and research collaborators and coauthors.

Selfe views the assessment process as one of increasing what Schön (1983) termed reflective professional practice, following the assumption that teachers that reflect on their own teaching will enjoy professional growth. The study "In the Long Run" (Walvoord, Hunt, Dowling, & McMahon, 1997), discussed in Chapter 5, evaluates the long term effects on disciplinary instructors of participation in WAC seminars.

Once the assessment has been conducted, the assessor is left with the problem of how to present the results. Haswell and McLeod (1997) address this with the following recommendations that will particularly assist those involved in assessment to be transmitted to administrators:

- Ask questions of the audience(s) before designing/beginning the assessment process in order to determine what information they value.

- Examine the genres of informational documents of the audience(s) and use them as models for the report.

- Focus on recommendations and action.

- Time the report(s) to coincide with appropriate points in the fiscal/budgetary cycle.

In their discussion of reporting assessment results, Haswell and McLeod wisely stress that the entire process and the resulting documents are, by nature, rhetorical. Consideration of purpose, context, *kairos* (timing), and audience are of paramount importance (p. 218).

11

WAC Classroom Practices–For Further Reading

By far the largest number of publications in Writing Across the Curriculum have been devoted to providing ideas for classroom writing activities in disciplines, ways of incorporating writing into curricular plans, and ways of supporting that writing while not losing focus on the disciplinary goals of courses. Instructors who regularly use writing in their classrooms, regardless of the discipline, report that they engage their students in composition practices that have been adapted to fit their discipline specific needs and goals. All disciplines are engaged in critical thinking, and critical thinking is at the heart of many of these practices: journaling, freewriting, peer review, reflective writing, writing to problem solve, micro-themes (Bean, et al., 1982), pre-test writing, written conference questions. However, teachers in each discipline select among these general activities to fit their needs, use these activities in particular ways to fit the subject area learning, and modify and develop new activities as the need arises. Because this literature is so extensive and lesson specific, we cannot provide a comprehensive review here, and we refer teachers to the following resources. We will follow that with discussion of sample publications arranged according to discipline, to give a flavor of the different ways disciplines have incorporated writing in their courses.

The best place to begin an investigation of discipline specific classroom writing practices is the WAC Clearinghouse (http://wac. colostate.edu/). Designed especially for ease of access, the WAC Clearinghouse is a resource that provides up-to-date on-line books, teacher exchange, and four journals for any educator interested in using writing in their classroom. The WAC Clearinghouse is a gateway to learning more about how to implement discipline specific practices for Writing Across the Curriculum. In addition to the resources at the site, there are well-maintained links to bibliographies, teaching resources, research, programs, organizations, and many other valuable up-to-date needs. Among the bibliographic sites linked there are

- CompPile <http://comppile.tamucc.edu/index.html> (which has an extensive searchable data base of publications in the teaching of writing);

- the Edison Initiative Writing Across the Curriculum Bibliographies <http://www.uwm.edu/letsci/edison/wn.html> (which gathers subject specific WAC links in many disciplines);

- the Language and Learning across the Curriculum Bibliography <http://www.sfasu.edu/lalac/bibliog.html>;

- The CCCC Bibliography of Composition and Rhetoric <http://www.ibiblio.org/cccc/>;

- Electronic Communication Across the Curriculum <http://wordsworth2.net/projects/ecac/ecacbk1.htm>; and

- The National Network of Writing Across the Curriculum Programs (Elementary-University) <http://wac.gmu.edu/national/network.html>.

The WAC Clearinghouse also provides electronic access to journals that provide a continuing resource of new ideas: *Language and Learning Across the Disciplines* and *Academic.writing*—now combined into *Across the Disciplines*—and *The WAC Journal*. Further, it offers electronic reprints of landmark books in writing across the curriculum as well as publishes new research and resources on composition and Writing Across the Curriculum, such as this book.

Some of the early print publications in WAC still provide many useful ideas for classrooms in different disciplines. Barbara Walvoord in 1982 (2nd ed. 1986) first published *Helping Students Write Well: A Guide for Teachers in all Disciplines,* which is still one of the most useful guides for disciplinary faculty new to writing. In the mid-1980s the National Education Association published a series of volumes on teaching writing in the content areas at the elementary, junior high school, high school, and college levels (Tchudi & Tchudi, 1983; Tchudi & Huerta, 1983; Tchudi & Yates, 1983; Tchudi, 1986). A 1982 collection edited by C.W. Griffin, *Teaching writing in all disciplines,* also provides a range of useful classroom ideas.

Andrew Moss and Carol Holder's (1988) *Improving Student Writing: A Guidebook for Faculty in All Disciplines* provides a compact introduction to many practical issues of introducing writing in all subject areas, along with sample activities and assignments. More recently, Farrell-Childers, Gere, & Young's (1994) *Programs and Practices: Writing Across the Secondary School Curriculum* and Margot Soven's (1996) *Write to Learn: A Guide to Writing Across the Curriculum* provide a similar introduction, while John Bean's (1996) *Engaging Ideas: The Professor's Guide to Integrating Writing, Critical Thinking, and Active Learning in the Classroom* provides a more in depth treatment.

Anson, Schwiebert, and Williamson's *Writing Across the Curriculum: An Annotated Bibliography* (1993), covers over 1000 items and provides comprehensive coverage through the early 1990s; over 600 of the items are pedagogic, arranged by subject area. Finally, the teaching journals in various disciplines, such as *Teaching of Psychology, The Journal of Economic Education,* and *The Journal of Teaching Sociology,* often contain articles about writing in the respective disciplines.

Mathematics

The 1989 collection *Writing to Learn Mathematics and Science,* edited by Connolly and Vilardi, Gopen and Smith, reports on the dichotomy between mathematics and writing as a "tradition in the American education system" (p. 209). It is no wonder they were surprised that a two-hour session on the topic of the use of writing in mathematics classes organized for the 1988 Mathematical Association of America meeting actually required three full sessions to accommodate everyone who wanted to present a paper: eight hours and thirty-six presentations. But even in 1988, writing to learn math was not a new idea. The 1989 Curriculum and Evaluation Standards for School Mathematics published by the National Council of Teachers of Mathematics set the direction for reform in mathematics teaching and learning as it endorsed the benefit of writing assignments in the mathematics classroom to enhance student understanding. In the face of this mathematics education reform, the focus of attention in the National Council of Teachers of Mathematics 1990 yearbook necessarily shifted from 1980s curricular issues and the teaching of specific content to the changing roles of students and teachers. The yearbook explores many writing to learn activities including journals, writing problems, and even letter writing to a friend to explain mathematics concepts, as effective methods of teaching (p. #). The editors have devoted a persuasive as well as practical chapter to writing as a tool for teaching mathematics, calling it the silent revolution. Writing in math class also encouraged and supported another math reform movement, collaborative learning.

1. The collection edited by Connolly and Vilardi (1989) presents many ways to develop students' conceptual understanding through writing, following a writing to learn philosophy. This collection surveys WAC classroom practices in middle school through college. Connolly claims informal classroom writing can help students to "retain natural curiosity; promote confidence in reason's ability to construct order by trial and error, even in problematic circumstances; and overcome anxiety that occurs when education stresses answers, not options, and product, not process" (p. 6). He explains that students, who don't succeed in math and science, have few tools and opportunities to think about those subjects. They have no language to even ask an "intelligent" question. Writing allows students to communicate what they think about how to do math and science, thereby making knowledge of it. The book presents these ways of using writing to learn in *Freewriting* at the beginning of class, to become present and centered, eliminating the distractions we bring to class.

2. *Focused freewriting* to cast a net of inquiry, initiating exploration of a term, issue, question, or problem.

3. *Attitudinal writing* to discover attitudes that affect aptitudes for learning by asking students: What expectation or experience do you bring to this reading? What difficulties did you have with the last assignment? What is most difficult for you at this point in the course? What do we need to do differently?

4. *Reflective, probative writing* to initiate or to conclude a class discussion or, mid-class, to refocus a discussion that is confused or lacks energy.

5. *"Meta-cognitive" process writing* to observe how one reads, takes an exam, works on a problem, writes a paper, thinks about an issue—writing that records one's own learning behavior, allowing one to become more autonomous and less reliant on the information and authority of teachers or texts.

6. *Explaining errors* on a test or homework—a particular type of "process writing" that helps students and teachers recognize where things went wrong and why.

7. *Questioning* while doing homework or at the end of class (another type of "process writing"), enabling students and teachers to recognize doubts, reservations, confusions, and uncertainties.

8. *Summarizing* what was said in a class or a reading.

9. *Defining*—substituting personal definitions, however imprecise, for memorization of textbook terms.

10. *Creating problems*—defining problems and issues of one's own, as an alternative to answering others' questions.

11. *Writing to read*—through double entry notebooks, reporting what an author says and, in a facing column, responding to it. Such dialectical notebooks integrate attitudinal writing, questioning, summarizing, and process writing.

12. *Learning logs, microthemes, paired problem solving,* and so forth.

The purposes of writing in the math classroom vary little across the grades even as classroom practices differ. In *Writing in Math Class: A Resource for Grades 2–8,* Marilyn Burns (1995) describes two purposes for writing in the elementary classroom: writing to support learning and writing to assess understanding. These fundamental WAC principles are demonstrated throughout this practical "how-to" guide as Burns provides examples of four categories of writing assignments and their assessment: "keeping journals or logs, solving math problems, explaining mathematical ideas, and writing about thinking processes"

(p. 49). Burns provides numerous examples of student work to demonstrate how they take up writing in the classroom and even provides ideas for "creative writing" assignments about math.

Reisch (2000) presents two writing assignments in developmental college math classes to build math confidence "through setting goals, considering and implementing strategies to attain these goals, and then reflecting on these experiences" (p. 1). In the first assignment (The Math Autobiography), students are asked to reflect upon and describe where they are coming from, where they are now, and where they are going. They are asked to set goals for themselves and identify strategies to help them achieve these goals. The second assignment (Course Reflection) continues the reflecting process. It asks students to look back on the semester and the writing they did in the Autobiography and to consider the following: What did I want to accomplish this semester? What did I do to insure my success? How can I build off of this experience in my next mathematics course? Autobiographies and reflective writing for goal setting are tools used widely in composition classrooms as well as in many of the other disciplines. Other useful ideas for writing in mathematics classes appear in Countryman, (1992) *Writing to learn mathematics: Strategies that work, K-12;* Drake & Amspaugh, (1994), "What writing reveals in mathematics," Cooney & Hirsch (1989), *Writing to learn Mathematics and Science,* and Gopen & Smith (1990) "What's an assignment like you do doing in a course like this?: Writing to learn mathematics."

English, Literature and Language Arts

Since the mid-1980s, the National Council of Teachers of English (NCTE) has published numerous volumes on classroom practice. The NCTE website (www.ncte.org) is rich in resources for the K-12 language arts or English teacher. This comprehensive site is easy to access and has grade specific lesson plans, journals, teacher talk, and current curricular information and is perhaps the single best WAC resource for the teaching of language arts and literature. Educators offer examples of uses of reflective writing, journaling, cross age tutoring, co-operative learning, summarizing, writing to read, and various meta-cognitive processes. In short, a survey of the kinds of lesson plans offered makes it clear that language arts makes use of the same tools as other disciplines. In fact, many of the kinds of lessons explained are easily adaptable to high school or college classrooms, using age appropriate content.

Recent publications such as *The Literature Workshop,* by Sheridan Blau (2003), exemplify the kinds of tools now at work in many high school and college literature classrooms. The book describes in detail how to conduct a literature workshop and provides the author's experiences in the classroom with his students as a benchmark for the kind of results that can be expected. The goals of the literature workshop are to "move students through a disciplined process of inquiry and reflection that will serve as a kind of initiatory and prototypical experience for them to refer to when confronted with future textual problems" (p. 32). The underlying assumptions of this text are shared by other disciplines that seek to incorporate writing to learn approaches because the teacher is no longer the repository of all information, writing to learn helps move students to a place of disciplinary competence in the absence of the teacher. Blau acknowledges that writing for the literature classroom is problematic for students because they aren't able to use writing about literature to construct knowledge. Blau recommends journals or logs as places students can experiment with analysis and criticism or to record questions or confusion about texts. These logs are then used as a catalyst for classroom discussion to build understanding of the text. Reading logs, reading process research reports, and an interpretation project are elements of the literature workshop that incorporate writing to learn tools.

Two articles appearing in Herrington and Moran's (1992) edited collection *Writing, Teaching, and Learning in the Disciplines* provide two strikingly different approaches to talking about the use of journals in literature classes. MacDonald and Cooper studied the effect of two different kinds of journal writing—dialogic and academic—on student learning in a literature classroom. Like a double entry notebook, the dialogic journal asks students to identify parts of a text to comment on and then to write reflectively about their initial observations. The academic journal focuses student writing on specific questions and problems and asks the student to make a claim supported by evidence. While they found that the academic journal improved student performance on latter critical essays, the dialogic journal had a negative impact, by leading students toward a diffuse personal style inappropriate for the assignment. In the same collection, Toby Fulwiler uses his own teaching journal to explain his use of dialogue journals, freewriting, small groups, peer review, three genres of papers, and multiple drafting and revision, in an American Literature class for non-majors. This experiential account offers a step-by-step reflection on how to implement this WAC strategy in a literature course. His experience was that these forms of writing made the course "both serious and exciting at the same time" (Fulwiler, 1992, p. 157).

Psychology

In her April 1985 article "Writing as a tool for teaching social psychology" published in *Teaching of Psychology,* Sara Snodgrass suggested the use of course logs (a kind of journal), writing analyses of published articles, and writing a formal research report based on observational study to teach psychology.

In *Writing and Psychology,* Vipond (1993b) focuses on the audience, genre, and style of writing in psychology. In his final chapter, Vipond suggests ways instructors can make writing a more vital part of students' academic lives. Vipond suggests less reliance on the textbook as the authority and more as a reference if students are to learn to write as authorities about the subject. He recommends journal writing to foster learning and communicating, allowing psychology students to examine their own ideas and experience, and not just those of others. He argues that the relationship between writer and reader be revitalized and that the audience metaphor (which implies performance) be replaced with the metaphor of conversation or dialogue. Furthermore, Vipond encourages instructors to be real readers and responders to student writing, rather than examiners and graders.

1. He offers some practical suggestions to incorporate writing into large classrooms: pairing a large lecture with a small writing intensive course as is done in the University of Washington Links program.

2. Using peer tutors and/or TAs in the classroom to assist with writing instruction and response.

3. Regularly assigning a 1-minute paper. At the end of class students write about the major point they learned that day and the one unanswered question they have. Papers are gathered and

used as the basis for the next lecture. Students learn that writing about psychology is a mode of learning about it.

4. Inkshedding. Students write about a topic and share with each other, thereby creating an atmosphere where writing is used, expected, and valued (Vipond, 1993b, p. 81).

Vipond's (1993a) "Social Motives for Writing Psychology: Writing for and with Younger Readers" examines the differences in how ninth graders and college level students understand various psychological concepts based on the findings from a cooperative writing project. By having his college class explain psychological concepts in writing to a ninth grade class, Vipond demonstrates how students can learn to adopt more authority in their writing about psychology.

In her 1994 *Teaching of Psychology* article "Lessons Learned from an Interdisciplinary Writing Course: Implications for Student Writing in Psychology," Dana Dunn recommends freewriting, small-group writing assignments, and peer tutoring as effective writing to learn methods in an interdisciplinary writing course, while she supports optional revision, peer feedback, and student assessment by more than one faculty evaluator. Sally Radmacher and Elizabeth Latosi-Sawin (1995) reported that in a case study students who participated in summary writing exercises scored better on final exams than non–participating students.

Economics

In 1991, the American Economic Association's report "The Status and Prospects of the Economics Major" suggested that the integration of writing into the teaching of economics would assist students in learning to think like economists. The most often employed tools for doing this, according to a survey, are the microtheme (students write a one-minute paper at the end of class to summarize their learning for the day) and recursive research paper assignments that include instructor and peer feedback as well as revision. Because writing is an important component of the professional life of an economist, learning argumentation strategies was identified as a goal of writing to learn assignments (Siegfried, et al., 1991).

Cohen and Spencer (1993), explain how an economics professor and a writing instructor restructured an upper-division economics course to focus on the writing process rather than the end product, with the goal of "getting students to think analytically and making arguments" (p. 223). They made no changes to course content, but substituted six different writing exercises for the in-class midterm, final exam, and 15–20 page term paper. This paper is an excellent and often cited example of how writing in the economics classroom promotes discipline specific critical thinking and learning and provides examples of writing assignments and student evaluation forms. Other ideas for writing in economics are contained in Tobey (1979), Crowe & Youga (1986), Henry (1986), Hansen (1993), Palmini (1996), McElroy (1997), Davidson & Gumnior (1993), Simpson & Carroll (1999), and Goma (2001).

History

Writing is of central importance to the study and practice of history, and there are hundreds of resources available on the relationship between history and writing in the classroom from the early 1980s to the present. The assumption that guides most historians who promote writing to learn about history is that writing about history encourages students to become more engaged with the topic and to learn to think like an historian. Classroom writing practices used most often in the teaching of history include journaling, warm-up freewriting exercises at the beginning of class, response writing to specific historical questions or problems, writing for different audiences and from different perspectives, and the use of microthemes to advance content understanding and encourage multiple drafts and revision rather than assigning the term paper. Because the discipline has emphasized writing to learn strategies, there are ample examples available of effective classroom practices. These include Beyer (1980), Brostoff & Beyer (1980), Holsinger (1983), Holsinger (1991), Steffens (1989), and Wyatt (2001).

Bibliography

Ackerman, J. (1993). The promise of writing to learn. *Written Communication, 10,* 334–370.

Adams, K. H. (1993). *A history of professional writing instruction in American colleges.* Dallas: Southern Methodist University Press.

Adler-Kassner, L. (1998). Ownership revisited: An exploration in progressive and expressivist composition scholarship. *College Composition and Communication, 49*(2), 208–231.

Amariglio, J. (1990). Economics as a postmodern discourse. In W. J. Samuels (Ed.), *Economics as discourse* (pp. 15–46). Norwell, MA: Kluwer.

Anson, C. M., Carter, M., Dannels, D. P., & Rust, J. (in press). Mutual support: CAC programs and institutional improvement in undergraduate ducation. *Across the Disciplines.*

Anson, C. M., Schwiebert, J. E., & Williamson, M. M. (1993). *Writing across the curriculum: An annotated bibliography.* Westport, CT: Greenwood Press.

Applebee, A. (1984). Writing and reasoning. *Review of Educational Research, 54,* 577–596.

Atkinson, D. (1999). *Scientific discourse in socio-historic context.* Mahwah, NJ: Erlbaum.

Atkinson, P. (1990). *The ethnographic imagination: Textual constructions of reality.* London: Routledge.

Atkinson, P. (1992). *Understanding ethnographic texts.* Newbury Park, CA: Sage.

Auden,W. H. (1962). *The Dyer's Hand and Other Essays.* New York: Random House.

Audet, R. H., Hickman, P., & Dobrynina, G. (1996). Learning logs: A classroom practice for enhancing scientific sense making. *Journal of Research in Science Teaching, 33,* 205–222.

Backhouse, R., Dudley-Evans, T., & Henderson, W. (Eds.). (1993). *Economics and language.* London: Routledge.

Bakhtin, M. (1986). *Speech genres and other late essays* (V. W. McGee, Trans.; C. Emerson & M. Holquist, Eds.). Austin: University of Texas Press.

Barnes, D., Britton, J., & Rosen, H. (1971). *Language, the learner and the school* (Rev. ed.), London: Penguin.

Barnett, R.W., & Blumner, J. (Eds.). (1999). *Writing centers and writing across the curriculum* programs: *Building interdisciplinary partnerships.* Westport, CT: Greenwood Press.

Bateson, G. (1958). *Naven, a survey of the problems suggested by a composite picture of the culture of a New Guinea tribe drawn from three points of view.* Stanford, CA: Stanford University Press.

Battalio, J. T. (1998a). *The rhetoric of science in the evolution of American ornithological discourse.* Stamford, CT: Ablex.

Battalio, J. T. (Ed.). (1998b). *Essays in the study of scientific discourse: Methods, practice, and pedagogy.* Stamford, CT: Ablex.

Bawarshi, A. (2000). The Genre Function. *College English, 62*(3), 327–352.

Bawarshi, A. (2001). The Ecology of Genre. In S. I. Dobrin & C. R. Weisser (Eds.), *Ecocomposition: Theoretical and Pedagogical Approaches* (pp. 69–80). New York: State University of New York Press.

Bawarshi, A. (2003). *Genre and the invention of the writer: Reconsidering the place of invention in composition.* Logan, UT: Utah State University Press.

Bazerman, C. (1980). A relationship between reading and writing: The conversational model. *College English, 41*(6), 656–661.

Bazerman, C. (1981). What written knowledge does: Three examples of academic discourse. *Philosophy of the Social Sciences* 11(3), 361–388.

Bazerman, C. (1984a). Modern evolution of the experimental report: Spectroscopic articles in Physical Review, 1893–1980. *Social Studies of Science, 14,* 163–196.

Bazerman, C. (1984b). The writing of scientific non-fiction: Contexts, choices and constraints. *Pre/Text, 5,* 39–74.

Bazerman, C. (1985). Physicists reading physics: Schema-laden purposes and purpose-laden schema. *Written Communication, 2,* 3–23.

Bazerman, C. (1987). Codifying the social scientific style. In J. S. Nelson, A. Megill, & D. N. McCloskey (Eds.), *The rhetoric of the human sciences: Language and argument in scholarship and public affairs* (pp. 125–144). Madison, WI: University of Wisconsin Press.

Bazerman, C. (1988). *Shaping written knowledge: The genre and activity of the experimental article in science.* Madison, WI: University of Wisconsin Press.

Bazerman, C. (1992). From cultural criticism to disciplinary participation: Living with powerful words. In A. Herrington & C. Moran (Eds.), *Writing, Teaching, and Learning in the Disciplines* (pp. 61–68). New York: MLA.

Bazerman, C. (1993). Money talks: The rhetorical project of the wealth of nations. In R. Backhouse, T. Dudley-Evans, & W. Henderson (Eds.), *Economics and language* (pp. 173–199). London: Routledge.

Bazerman, C. (1994). *Constructing experience.* Carbondale, IL: Southern Illinois Press.

Bazerman, C. (1995). *The informed writer.* (5th ed.). Boston: Houghton Mifflin.

Bazerman, C. (1997). Discursively structured activities. *Mind, Culture, and Activity, 4*(4), 296–308.

Bazerman, C. (1999). *The languages of Edison's light.* Cambridge, MA: MIT Press.

Bazerman, C. (2002). Distanced and refined selves: Educational tensions in writing with the power of knowledge. In *Academic writing in context* (pp. 23–29). Birmingham: University of Birmingham Press.

Bazerman, C. (in press). Intertextualities: Volosinov, Bakhtin, literary theory, and literacy studies. In A. Ball & S. Freedman (Eds.), *New Literacies for New Times.* Cambridge: Cambridge University Press.

Bazerman, C., & Paradis, J. (Eds.). (1991). *Textual dynamics of the professions: Historical and contemporary studies of writing in professional communities.* Madison, WI: University of Wisconsin Press.

Bazerman, C., & Russell, D. R. (Eds.). (1994). *Landmark essays on writing across the curriculum.* Davis, CA: Hermagoras Press.

Bazerman, C., & Russell, D. R. (Eds.). (2003). *Writing selves/writing societies: Research from activity perspectives: Perspectives on writing.* Fort Collins, CO: The WAC Clearinghouse. [On-line]. Available: http://wac.colostate.edu/books/selves_societies/

Bean, J. (1996). *Engaging ideas: The professor's guide to integrating writing, critical thinking, and active learning in the classroom.* San Francisco: Jossey-Bass.

Bean, J. C. (1983). Computerized word-processing as an aid to revision. *College Composition and Communication, 34,* 146–148.

Bean, J. C., Drenk, D., & Lee, F. D. (1982). Microtheme strategies for developing cognitive skills. In *Teaching Writing in All Disciplines* (pp. 27–38). San Francisco: Jossey-Bass.

Becker, H. S. (1986). *Writing for social scientists: How to start and finish your thesis, book, or article.* Chicago: University of Chicago Press.

Becker, H. S. (1998). *Tricks of the trade: How to think about your research while you're doing it.* Chicago: University of Chicago Press.

Beins, B. C. (1993). Writing assignments in statistics classes encourage students to learn interpretation. *Teaching of Psychology, 20,* 161–164.

Belanoff, P., Elbow, P., & Fontaine, S. L. (Eds.). (1991). *Nothing begins with N: New investigations of freewriting.* Carbondale, IL: Southern Illinois University Press.

Bennett, J. (1981). *Oral history and delinquency: The rhetoric of criminology.* Chicago: University of Chicago Press.

Benton, R. (1990). A hermeneutic approach to economics. In W. J. Samuels (Ed.), *Economics as discourse* (pp. 65–89). Norwell, MA: Kluwer.

Berkenkotter, C. (2001). Genre systems at work: DSM-IV and rhetorical recontextualization in Psychotherapy Paperwork. *Written Communication, 18*(3), 326–349.

Berkenkotter, C. (2002). Capturing insanity: The wedding of photography and physiognomy in the nineteenth century medical journal article. In P. J. Coppock (Ed.), *The Semiotics of Writing: Transdisciplinary Perspectives on theTechnology of Writing* (pp. 205–229). Tornhout, Belgium: Brepols.

Berkenkotter, C., & Huckin, T. (1995). *Genre knowledge in disciplinary communication: Cognition/culture/power.* Hillsdale, NJ: Erlbaum.

Berkenkotter, C., & Ravotas, D. (1997) Genre as tool in the transmission of practice over time and across disciplinary boundaries. *Mind, Culture, and Activity, 4*(4), 256–274.

Berkenkotter, C., & Ravotas, D. (1998). Voices in the text: Varieties of reported speech in psychotherapists' initial assessments. *Text: An Interdisciplinary Journal for the Study of Discourse,18*(2), 211–239.

Berkenkotter, C., & Ravotas, D. (2001). New research strategies in genre analysis: Reported speech as recontextualization in a psychotherapist's notes and psychosocial assessment. In E. Barton & G. Stygall (Eds.), *Discourse studies and composition studies* (pp. 223–249). Cresskill, NJ: Hampton Press.

Berkenkotter, C., & Ravotas, D. (2002). Psychotherapists as authors: Microlevel analysis of therapists' written reports. In J. Z. Sadler (Ed.), *Descriptions and prescriptions: values, mental disorders, and the DSMs* (pp. 251–268). Baltimore: Johns Hopkins University Press.

Berman, R. (1978, October 2). Stamping out illiteracy. *Chronicle of Higher Education,* p. 72.

Beyer, B. (1980). Using writing to learn in history. *History Teacher,* 13(2), 167–178.

Bhatia, V. (1993). *Analysing genre: Language use in professional settings.* London: Longman.

Biagioli, M. (1993). *Galileo, courtier: The practice of science in the culture of absolutism.* Chicago: University of Chicago Press.

Biggs, J. B., & Collis, K. F. (1991). Multimodal learning and quality of intelligent behavior. In H. H. Rowe (Ed.), *Intelligence: Reconceptualization and measurement* (pp. 57–66). Hillsdale, NJ: Erlbaum.

Bitzer, L. (1968). The rhetorical situation. *Philosophy and Rhetoric, 1,* 1–14.

Blakeslee, A. M. (1997). Activity, context, interaction, and authority: Learning to write scientific papers. *Journal of Business and Technical Communication, 11*(2), 125–169.

Blakeslee, A. M. (2001). *Interacting with audiences.* Mahwah, NJ: Erlbaum.

Blau, S. (2003). *The literature workshop: Teaching texts and their readers.* Portsmouth, NH: Heinemann.

Bowen, B. A. (1994). Telecommunications networks: Expanding the contexts for literacy. In C. L. Selfe & S. Hilligoss (Eds.), *Literacy and computers: The complications of teaching and learning with technology* (pp. 113–129). New York: MLA.

Brereton, J. C. (Ed.). (1995). *The origins of composition studies in the American college, 1875–1925: A documentary history.* Pittsburgh: University of Pittsburgh Press.

Bretzing, B., & Kulhavy, R. (1979). Notetaking and depth of processing. *Contemporary Educational Psychology, 4,* 145–153.

Britton, J. (1970). *Language and learning.* Portsmouth, NH: Boynton/Cook.

Britton, J., Burgess, T., Martin, N., McLeod, A., & Rosen, H. (1975). *The development of writing ablities (11–18).* London: Macmillan.

Brostoff, A., & Beyer, B. (1980). An approach to integrating writing into a history course. *Journal of Basic Writing, 2*(4), 36–52.

Brown, R. H. (1977). *A poetic for sociology: Toward a logic of discovery for the human sciences.* Cambridge: Cambridge University Press.

Brown, R. H. (1987). *Society as text: Essays on rhetoric, reason, and reality.* Chicago: University of Chicago Press.

Brown, R. H. (1989). *Social science as civic discourse: Essays on the invention, legitimation, and uses of social theory.* Chicago: University of Chicago Press.

Brown, R. H. (Ed.). (1992). *Writing the social text: Poetics and politics in social science discourse.* New York: A. de Gruyter.

Brown, V. (1994). *Adam Smith's discourse.* London: Routledge.

Bruffee, K. A. (1984). Collaborative learning and the "conversation of mankind." *College English, 46,* 635–652.

Bruner, J. S. (1963). *The process of education.* Westminster, MD: Random.

Bruner, J. S. (1964). *On knowing: Essays for the left hand.* Cambridge, MA: Belknap Press of Harvard University Press.

Bruner, J. S. (1986). *Actual minds, possible worlds.* Cambridge: Harvard UP.

Bullock, A. (1975). *A language for life: Report of the committee of inquiry appointed by the secretary of state for education and science under the chairmanship of Sir Alan Bullock.* London: Her Majesty's Stationery Office.

Burke, K. (1945). *A grammar of motives.* New York: Prentice Hall.

Burns, M. (1995). *Writing in math class: A resource for grades 2–8.* Sausalito, CA: Math Solutions Publications.

Campbell, J. A. (1974). Charles Darwin and the crisis of ecology: A rhetorical perspective. *Quarterly Journal of Speech, 60,* 442–449.

Campbell, J. A. (1975). The polemical Mr. Darwin. *Quarterly Journal of Speech, 61,* 375–390.

Campbell, J. A. (1986). Scientific revolution and the grammar of culture: The case of Darwin's origin. *Quarterly Journal of Speech, 72,* 351–376.

Campbell, J. A. (1989). The invisible rhetorician: Charles Darwin's "third party" strategy. *Rhetorica, 7,* 55–85.

Campbell, O. J. (1939). The failure of freshman English. *English Journal, 28,* 177–185.

Cannon, R. E. (1990). Experiments with writing to teach microbiology. *American Biology Teacher, 52*(3), 156–158.

Carleton College. (1975). Teaching writing extra-territorially. *ADE Bulletin, 44,* 32ff.

Carter, M. (2002). A process for establishing outcomes-based assessment plans for writing and speaking in the disciplines. *Language and Learning Across the Disciplines, 6,* 4–29.

Carter, M., Anson, C. M., & Miller, C. R. (in press). Assessing technical writing in institutional contexts: Using outcomes-based assessment for programmatic thinking." *Technical Communication Quarterly.*

Casanave, C. P. (1992). Cultural diversity and socialization: A case of a Hispanic woman in a doctoral program in sociology. In D. E. Murry (Ed.), *Diversity as a Resource: Redefining cultural literacy* (pp. 148–182). Alexandria, VA: TESOL.

Casanave, C. P. (1995). Local interactions: Constructing contexts for composing in a graduate sociology program. In D. Belcher & G. Braine (Eds.), *Academic writing in a second language: Essays on research and pedagogy* (pp. 83–110). Norwood, NJ: Ablex.

Casanave, C. P. (2002). *Writing games: Multicultural case studies of academic literacy practices in higher education.* Mahwah, NJ: Erlbaum.

Charney, D. (1994). The effect of hypertext on processes of reading and writing. In C. L. Selfe & S. Hilligoss (Eds.), *Literacy and computers: The complications of teaching and learning with technology* (pp. 238–263). New York: MLA.

Chinn, P. W. U., & Hilgers, T. L. (2000). From corrector to collaborator: The range of instructor roles in writing-based natural and applied science classes. *Journal of Research in Science Teaching, 37,* 3–25.

Chiseri-Strater, E. (1991). *Academic literacies: The public and private discourse of university students.* Portsmouth, NH: Boynton/Cook.

Christie, F. (1985). Language and schooling. In S. Tschudi (Ed.), *Language, schooling, and society.* Upper Montclair, NJ: Boynton/Cook.

Clifford, J. (1980). Fieldwork, reciprocity and the making of ethnographic texts. *Man, 15,* 518–532.

Clifford, J. (1983). On ethnographic authority. *Representations, 1*(2), 118–146.

Clifford, J., & Marcus, G. E. (Eds.). (1986). *Writing culture: The poetics and politics of ethnography.* Berkeley: University of California Press.

Coe, R., Lingard, L., & Teslenko, T. (2002). *The rhetoric and ideology of genre: Strategies for stability and change.* Cresskill, NJ: Hampton Press.

Cohen, A. J., & Spencer, J. (1993). Integrating Writing Across the Curriculum into Economics: A Case Study, Benefits, and Costs. *Journal of Economic Education, 24,* 219–230.

Coker, F. H., & Scarboro, A. (1990). Writing to learn in upper-division sociology courses: Two case studies. *Teaching Sociology, 18*(2), 218–222.

Cole, M. (1996). *Cultural psychology.* Cambridge: Harvard University Press.

Collins, H. (1985). *Changing order: Replication and induction in scientific practice.* Beverly Hills: Sage.

Collins, H., & Pinch, T. (1982). *Frames of meaning: The social construction of extraordinary science.* London: Routledge & Kegan Paul.

Committee on College English, NCTE. (1935). *The teaching of college English.* New York: Appleton-Century.

Connolly, P., & Vilardi, T. (1989). *Writing to learn mathematics and science.* New York: Teachers College Press.

Connor, U. (1996). *Contrastive rhetoric: Cross-cultural aspects of second-language writing.* Cambridge: Cambridge University Press.

Connor, U., & Kaplan, R. (Eds.). (1987). *Writing across languages: Analysis of L2 text.* Reading, MA: Addison-Wesley.

Connors, R. (1991). Rhetoric in the modern university: The creation of an underclass. In R. Bullock & J. Trimbur (Eds.), *The politics of writing instruction: Postsecondary* (pp. 55–84). Portsmouth, NH: Boynton/Cook.

Connors, R. (1995). The new abolitionism: Toward a historical background. In J. Petraglia (Ed.), *Reconceiving writing, rethinking writing instruction* (pp. 3–26). Mahwah, NJ: Erlbaum.

Cooney, T. J., & Hirsch, C. R. (Eds.). (1989). *Writing to learn mathematics and science.* New York: Teachers College Press.

Cooper, M. M., & Selfe, C. L. (1990). Computer conferences and learning: Authority, resistance, and internally persuasive discourse. *College English, 52,* 847–869.

Cope, B., & Kalantzis, M. (Eds.). (1993). *The powers of literacy: A genre approach to teaching writing.* London: Falmer Press.

Countryman, J. (1992). *Writing to learn mathematics: Strategies that work.* Portsmouth, NH: Heinemann.

Cowles, K. V., Strickland, D., & Rodgers, B. L. (2001). Collaboration for teaching innovation: Writing across the curriculum in a school of nursing. *Journal of Nursing Education, 40,* 363–367.

Cozzens, S. (1985). Comparing the sciences: Citation context analysis of papers from neuropharmacology and the sociology of science. *Social Studies of Science, 15,* 127–153.

Crapanzano, V. (1976). On the writing of ethnography. *Dialectical Anthropology, 2,* 69–73.

Crapanzano, V. (1977). The life history in anthropological field work. *Anthropology and Humanism Quarterly, 2,* 3–7.

Crowe, D., & Youga, J. (1986). Using writing as a tool for learning economics. *Journal of Economic Education, 17,* 218–222.

Daiute, C. (1983). The computer as stylus and audience. *College Composition and Communication, 34,* 134–145.

Daly, J., & Miller, M. (1975). The empirical development of an instrument to measure writing apprehension. *Research in the Teaching of English, 12,* 242–249.

Davidson, L. S., & Gumnior, E. C. (1993). Writing to learn in a business economics class. *Journal of Economic Education, 24*(3), 237–243.

Deans, T. (2000). *Writing partnerships: Service-learning in composition.* Urbana, IL: NCTE.

Dear, P. (1985). Totius in verba: Rhetoric and authority in the early royal society. *Isis, 76,* 145–161.

Dear, P. (1987). Jesuit mathematical science and the reconstruction of experience in the early seventeenth century. *Studies in the History and Philosophy of Science, 18,* 133–175.

Dear, P. (1990). Miracles, experiments and the ordinary course of nature. *Isis, 81,* 663–683.

Dear, P. (Ed.). (1991). *The literary structure of scientific argument: Historical studies.* Philadelphia: University of Pennsylvania Press.

Delpit, L. (1993). The politics of teaching literate discourse. In T. Perry & J. W. Fraser (Eds.), *Freedom's plough: Teaching in the multicultural classroom* (pp. 285–295). New York: Routledge.

Devitt, A. (1991). Intertextuality in tax accounting: Generic, referential, and functional. In C. Bazerman & J. Paradis (Eds.), *Textual dynamics of the professions* (pp. 336–380). Madison, WI: University of Wisconsin Press.

Di Vesta, F., & Gray, G. (1972). Listening and notetaking. *Journal of Educational Psychology, 63,* 8–14.

Dias, P., Pare, A., Freedman, A., & Medway, P. (1999). *Worlds apart: Acting and writing in academic and workplace contexts.* Mahwah, NJ: Erlbaum.

Dixon, J. (1967). *Growth through English: A report based on the Dartmouth seminar, 1966.* Reading, UK: National Association for the Teaching of English.

Drake, R. M., & Amspaugh, L. B. (1994). What writing reveals in mathematics. *Focus on learning problems in mathematics, 16*(3), 43–50.

Dudley-Evans, T., & Henderson, W. (Eds.). (1990). *The language of economics: The analysis of economics discourse.* Britain: Modern English.

Duin, A. H., & Hansen, C. (1994). Reading and writing on computer networks as social construction and social interaction. In C. L. Selfe & S. Hilligoss (Eds.), *Literacy and computers: The complications of teaching and learning with technology* (pp. 89–112). New York: MLA.

Duke, C. R., & Sanchez, R. (Eds.). (2001). *Assessing writing across the curriculum.* Durham, NC: Carolina Academic Press.

Dunn, D. S. (1994). Lessons learned from an interdisciplinary writing course: Implications for student writing in psychology. *Teaching of Psychology, 21*(4), 223–227.

Dunn, D. S. (1996). Collaborative writing in a statistics and research methods course. *Teaching of Psychology, 23*(1), 38–40.

Duran, J. (1998). *Philosophies of science/Feminist theories.* Boulder, CO: Westview.

Dysthe, O. (1996). The multivoiced classroom: Interactions of writing and classroom discourse. *Written Communication, 13*(3), 385–425.

Elbow, P. (1973). *Writing without teachers.* New York: Oxford University Press.

Elbow, P. (1998). Reflections on academic discourse: How it relates to freshmen and colleagues. In V. Zamel & R. Spack (Eds.), *Negotiating academic literacies: Teaching and learning across languages and cultures* (pp. 145–170). Mahwah, NJ: Erlbaum.

Emig, J. (1971). *The composing processes of twelfth graders.* Urbana, IL: NCTE.

Emig, J. (1977). Writing as a mode of learning. *College Composition and Communication, 28,* 122–128.

Emmerich, P. J. (1968). Written composition outside the English class. *Journal of English Teaching Techniques, 1*(4), 5–8.

Engestrom, Y. (1996). The tensions of judging: Handling cases of drunk driving under the influence of alcohol in Finland and California. In Y. Engestrom & D. Middleton (Eds.), *Cognition and communication at work* (pp. 199–232). Cambridge: Cambridge University Press.

Eurich, A. (1932). Should freshman composition be abolished? *English Journal, 21,* 208- 312.

Fahnestock, J. (1999). *Rhetorical figures in science.* New York: Oxford University Press.

Fahnestock, J., & Secor, M. (1991). The rhetoric of literary criticism. In C. Bazerman & J. Paradis (Eds.), *Textual dynamics of the professions: Historical and contemporary studies of writing in professional communities* (pp. 76–98). Madison, WI: University of Wisconsin Press.

Faigley, L., & Hansen, K. (1985). Learning to write in the social sciences. *College Composition and Communication, 36*(2), 140–149.

Farrell-Childers, P., Gere, A. R., & Young, A. (Eds.). (1994). *Programs and practices: Writing across the secondary school curriculum.* Portsmouth, NH: Boynton/Cook.

Farris, C., & Smith, R. (1992). Writing intensive courses: Tools for curricular change. In S. McLeod & M. Soven (Eds.), *Writing across the cur-*

riculum: A guide to developing programs (pp. 52–62). Newbury Park, CA: Sage Publications.

Fisher, J., & Harris, M. (1973). Effects of notetaking and review on recall. *Journal of Educational Psychology, 65,* 321–325.

Fishman, S. M. (1993). Explicating our tacit tradition: John Dewey and composition studies. *College Composition and Communication, 44*(3), 315–330.

Fishman, S. M., & McCarthy, L. P. (1992). Is expressivism dead? Reconsidering its romantic roots and its relations to social constructionism. *College English, 56*(6), 647–661.

Fishman, S. M., & McCarthy, L. P. (1995). Community in the expressivist classroom: Juggling liberal and communitarian visions. *College English, 57*(1), 62- 81.

Fishman, S. M., & McCarthy, L. P. (1996). Teaching for student change: A Deweyan alternative to radical pedagogy. *College Composition and Communication, 47*(3), 342–366.

Fishman, S. M., & McCarthy, L. P. (1998). *John Dewey and the challenge of classroom practice.* New York: Teachers College Press.

Fishman, S. M., & McCarthy, L. P. (2000). *Unplayed tapes.* New York: Teachers College Press.

Flower, L., Stein, V., Ackerman, J., Kantz, M. J., & McCormick, K. (1990). *Reading-to-write: Exploring a cognitive and social process.* New York: Oxford University Press.

Freedman, A., Adam, C., & Smart, G. (1994). Wearing suits to class: Simulating genres and simulations as genre. *Written Communication, 11*(2), 193–226.

Freedman, A., & Medway, P. (Eds.). (1994a). *Genre and the new rhetoric.* London: Taylor & Francis.

Freedman, A., & Medway, P. (Eds.). (1994b). *Learning and teaching genre.* Portsmouth, NH: Boynton/Cook.

Fuller, S. (1988). *Social epistemology.* Bloomington, IN: Indiana University Press.

Fuller, S. (1993). *Philosophy, rhetoric, and the end of knowledge: The coming of science and technology studies.* Madison, WI: University of Wisconsin Press.

Fulwiler, T. (1984). How well does writing across the curriculum work? *College Composition and Communication 46*(2), 113–125.

Fulwiler, T. (1987a). *The journal book.* Portsmouth, NH: Boynton/Cook.

Fulwiler, T. (1987b). *Teaching with writing.* Upper Montclair, NJ: Boynton/Cook.

Fulwiler, T. (1992). Writing and learning American literature. In A. Herrington & C. Moran (Eds.), *Writing, teaching, and learning in the disciplines* (pp. 156–173). New York: MLA.

Fulwiler, T., & Young, A. (1982). *Language connections: Writing and reading across the curriculum.* Urbana, IL: NCTE.

Fulwiler, T., & Young, A. (Eds.). (1990). *Programs that work: Models and methods for writing across the curriculum.* Portsmouth, NH: Boynton/Cook.

Fulwiler, T., & Young, A. (1997). Preface—the WAC archives revisited. In K. B. Yancey & B. Huot (Eds.), *Assessing writing across the curriculum: Diverse approaches and practices* (pp. 1–7). Greenwich, CT: Ablex.

Gaonkar, D. P. (1990). Rhetoric and its double: Reflections on the rhetorical turn in the human sciences. In H. Simons (Ed.), *The rhetorical turn: Invention and persuasion in the conduct of inquiry* (pp. 341–366). Chicago: University of Chicago Press.

Gardner, S., & Fulwiler, T. (1998). *The journal book for teachers in technical and professional programs.* Westport, CT: Boynton.

Gates, B., & Shtier, A. B. (Eds.). (1997). *Natural eloquence: Women reinscribe sciences.* Madison, WI: University of Wisconsin Press.

Geertz, C. (1973). *The interpretation of cultures: Selected essays.* New York: Basic Books.

Geertz, C. (1976). *The religion of Java.* Chicago: University of Chicago Press.

Geertz, C. (1980). *Negara: The theatre state in nineteenth-century Bali.* Princeton, NJ: Princeton University Press.

Geertz, C. (1983). *Local knowledge: Further essays in interpretive anthropology.* New York: Basic Books.

Geertz, C. (1988). *Works and lives: The anthropologist as author.* Stanford, CA: Stanford University Press.

Geisler, C. (1994). *Academic literacy and the nature of expertise: Reading, writing, and knowing in academic philosophy.* Hillsdale, NJ: Erlbaum.

George, D. (1990). The rhetoric of economics texts. *Journal of Economic Issues, 24,* 861–878.

Gieryn, T. (1983). Boundary-work and the demarcation of science from non-science: Strains and interests in professional ideologies of scientists. *American Sociological Review, 48,* 781–795.

Gieryn, T. (1999). *Cultural boundaries of science: Credibility on the line.* Chicago: University of Chicago Press.

Gilbert, N. (1977). Referencing as persuasion. *Social Studies of Science, 7,* 113–122.

Gilbert, G. N., & Mulkay, M. (1984). *Opening Pandora's box.* Cambridge: Cambridge University Press.

Gillis, A. (2001). Journal writing in health education. In L. English & M. Gillen (Eds.), *Promoting journal writing in adult education* (pp. 49–59). San Francisco: Jossey-Bass.

Golinski, J. (1992). *Science as public culture: Chemistry and enlightenment in Britain, 1760 1820.* Cambridge: Cambridge University Press.

Goma, O. D. (2001). Creative Writing in Economics. *College Teaching, 49*(4),149–152.

Gooding, D. (1990). *Experiment and the making of meaning: Human agency in scientific observation and experiment.* Dordrecht: Kluwer.

Gopen, G., & Smith, D. (1990). What's an assignment like you do doing in a course like this? Writing to learn mathematics. *The College Mathematics Journal, 21,* 2-19.

Gorman, M., Gorman, M., & Young, A. (1986). Poetic writing in psychology. In A. Young & T. Fulwiler (Eds.), *Writing across the disciplines: Research into practice* (pp. 139–159). Upper Montclair, NJ: Boynton/Cook.

Gould, S. J., & Lewontin, R. C. (1979). The spandrels of San Marco and the Panglossian paradigm: A critique of the adaptationist program. *Proceedings of the Royal Society of London B, 205,* 581–598.

Greene, S. (1993). The role of task in the development of academic thinking through reading and writing in a college history course. *Research in the Teaching of English, 27,* 37–48.

Griffin, C. W. (Ed.). (1982). *Teaching writing in all disciplines.* San Francisco: Jossey-Bass.

Gross, A. G. (1984). Style and arrangement in scientific prose. *Journal of Technical Writing and Communication 14,* 241–253.

Gross, A. G. (1985). The form of the experimental paper. *Journal of Technical Writing and Communication 15,* 15–26.

Gross, A. G. (1988). Discourse on method: The rhetorical analysis of scientific texts. *Pre/Text, 9,* 169–186.

Gross, A. G. (1990). *The rhetoric of science.* Cambridge: Harvard University Press.

Gross, A. G., & Keith, W. M. (Eds.). (1997). *Rhetorical hermeneutics: Invention and interpretation in the age of science.* Albany, NY: SUNY Press.

Gunnarsson, B. (1997). The writing process from a sociolinguistic viewpoint. *Written Communication, 14*(2), 139–188.

Gusfield, J. (1976). The literary rhetoric of science: Comedy and pathos in drinking driver research. *American Sociological Review, 41,* 16–34.

Gusfield, J. (1981). *The culture of public problems: drinking-driving and the symbolic order.* Chicago: University of Chicago Press.

Haas, C. (1993). Beyond "just the facts": Reading as rhetorical action. In A. M. Penrose & B. M. Sitko (Eds.), *Hearing ourselves think: Cognitive research in the college writing classroom* (pp. 19–32). New York: Oxford University Press.

Haas, C. (1994). Learning to read biology: One student's rhetorical development in college. *Written Communication, 11*(1), 43–84.

Haas, C. (1996). *Writing technology: Studies in the materiality of writing.* Mahwah, NJ: Erlbaum.

Halasek, K. (1999). *A pedagogy of possibility: Bakhtinian perspectives on composition studies.* Carbondale: Southern Illinois University Press.

Halliday, M. A. K. (1985). *An Introduction to functional grammar.* London: Edward Arnold.

Halliday, M. A. K., & Martin, J. R. (1993). *Writing science: Literacy and discursive power.* Pittsburgh: University of Pittsburgh Press.

Hand, B., & Prain, V. (2002). Teachers implementing writing-to-learn strategies in junior secondary science: A case study. *Science Education, 86,* 737–755.

Hand, B., Prain, V., & Wallace, C. (2002). Influences of writing tasks on students' answers to recall and higher-level test questions. *Research in Science Education, 32,* 19–34.

Hand, B., Wallace, C., & Yang, E. (in press). Using the science writing heuristic to enhance learning outcomes from laboratory activities in seventh grade science: Quantitative and qualitative aspects. *International Journal of Science Education.*

Hansen, W. L. (1993). Teaching a writing intensive course in economics. *Journal of Economic Education, 24*(3), 213–218.

Harding, S. (1986). *The science question in feminism.* Ithaca, NY: Cornell University Press.

Harding, S. (Ed.). (1987). *Feminism and methodology.* Bloomington: Indiana University Press.

Harding, S. (1998). *Is science multicultural?* Bloomington, IN: Indiana University Press.

Harding, S. (Ed.). (1993). *The "racial" economy of science.* Bloomington: Indiana University Press.

Harklau, L., Losey, K., & Siegal, M. (Eds.). (1999). *Generation 1.5 meets college composition: Issues in the teaching of writing to U.S.-educated learners of ESL.* Mahwah, NJ: Erlbaum.

Harris, M. (1998). Using computers to expand the role of writing centers. In D. Reiss, D. Selfe, & A. Young (Eds.), *Electronic communication across the curriculum* (pp. 3–16). Urbana, IL: NCTE.

Hartman, J. D. (1989). Writing to learn and communicate in a data structures course. *SIGCSE Bulletin, 21*(1), 32–36.

Hasan, J. R., & Martin, J. (1989). *Language development: learning language, learning culture.* Norwood, NJ: Ablex.

Haswell, R., & McLeod, S. (1997). WAC assessment and internal audiences: A dialogue. In K. B. Yancey & B. Huot (Eds.). *Assessing writing across the curriculum: Diverse approaches and practices* (pp. 217–236). Greenwich, CT: Ablex.

Hawisher, G. E. (1994). Blinding insights: Classification schemes and software for literacy instruction. In C. L. Selfe & S. Hilligoss (Eds.), *Literacy and computers: The complications of teaching and learning with technology* (pp. 37–55). New York: MLA.

Hawisher, G. E., LeBlanc, P., Moran, C., & Selfe, C. L. (1996). *Computers and the teaching of writing in American higher education, 1979–1994: A history.* Norwood, NJ: Ablex.

Heilbroner, R. L. (1990). Economics as ideology. In W. J. Samuels (Ed.), *Economics as discourse* (pp. 101–116). Norwell, MA: Kluwer.

Henry, L. H. (1986). Clustering: Writing (and learning) about economics. *College Teaching, 34*(3), 89–93.

Herrington, A. J. (1981). Writing to learn: Writing across the disciplines. *College English, 43,* 379–387.

Herrington, A. J. (1985). Writing in academic settings: A study of the contexts for writing in two college chemical engineering courses. *Research in the Teaching of English, 19,* 331–361.

Herrington, A. J. (1988). Teaching, writing, and learning: A naturalistic study of writing in an undergraduate literature course. In D. A. Jolliffe (Ed.), *Writing in academic disciplines: Advances in writing research* (Vol. 2) (pp.133–166), Norwood, NJ: Ablex.

Herrington, A. J., & Curtis, M. (2000). *Persons in Process,* Urbana IL: NCTE.

Herrington, A., & Moran, C. (Eds.). (1992). *Writing, teaching, and learning in the disciplines.* New York: MLA.

Hoffmann, R. (1988). Under the surface of the chemical article. *Angewandte Chemie International Edition English, 27,* 1593–1602.

Hoffmann, R. (2002). Writing (and drawing) chemistry. In J. Monroe (Ed.), *Writing and Revising the Disciplines* (pp. 29–53). Ithaca, NY: Cornell University Press.

Hoffmann, R., & Laszlo, P. (1991). Representation in Chemistry. *Angewandte Chemie International Edition English, 30,* 1–16.

Holdstein, D. H., & Bleich, D. (Eds.). (2001). *Personal effects: The social character of scholarly writing.* Logan, UT: Utah State University Press.

Holsinger, D. (1983). Writing to learn history. In C. Thaiss (Ed.), *Writing to Learn* (pp. 49-55). Dubuque, IA: Kendall/Hunt.

Holsinger, D. (1991). Writing to learn history. *Social Studies Review,* 59-64.

Hubbuch, S. M. (1996). *Writing research papers across the curriculum* (4th ed.). Fort Worth, TX: Harcourt Brace College Publishers.

Huckin, T. N., & Olsen, L. A. (1991). *Technical writing and professional communication for nonnative speakers of English.* New York: McGraw Hill.

Huff, S. (1974, November 29). Letters: Crisis in English composition. *Chronicle of Higher Education,* 12.

Hughes-Wiener, G., & Jensen-Cekalla, S. K. (1991). Organizing a WAC evaluation project: Implications for program planning. In L. C. Stanley & J. Ambron (Eds.). *Writing across the curriculum in community colleges: New directions for community colleges, No. 73.* (pp. 65–70), San Francisco: Jossey-Bass..

Hult, C. A. (1996). *Researching and writing: Across the curriculum.* Boston: Allyn & Bacon.

Humes, A. (1983). Research on the composing process. *Review of Educational Research, 53*(2), 201–216.

Huot, B. (1997). Preface—the WAC archives revisited. In K. B. Yancey & B. Huot (Eds.), *Assessing writing across the curriculum: Diverse approaches and practices.* (pp. 1–7). Greenwich, CT: Ablex.

Hyland, K. (2000*). Disciplinary discourses: Social interactions in academic writing.* New York: Longman.

Johns, A. (1998). *The nature of the book: Print and knowledge in the making.* Chicago: University of Chicago Press.

Johns, A. M. (1991). Interpreting an English competency examination: The frustrations of an ESL science student. *Written Communication, 8,* 379–401.

Johns, A. M. (2001). ESL students and WAC Programs: Varied students and diverse needs. In McCleod, et al. (Eds.), *WAC for the new millenium* (pp. 141–164). Urbana IL: NCTE.

Johns, A. M. (Ed.). (2002). *Genre in the classroom: Multiple perspectives.* Mahwah, NJ: Erlbaum.

Johns, J. L., & Lenski, S. D. (1997). *Improving reading: A handbook of strategies* (2nd ed.). Dubuque, IA: Kendall/Hunt.

Johnson, T. M., Jones, G., A., Thornton, C. A., Langrall, C. W., & Rous, A. (1998). Students' thinking and writing in the context of probability. *Written Communication, 15*(2), 203–229.

Johnstone, A. C., Johnstone, B., & Balester, V. M. (1994). *Uses for journal keeping: An ethnography of writing in a university science class.* Norwood, NJ: Ablex.

Jolliffe, D. (2001). Writing across the curriculum and service learning: Kairos, genre and collaboration. In S. McLeod, et al. (Eds.), *WAC for the new millennium* (pp. 179–199). Urbana IL: NCTE.

Jolliffe, D., & Brier, E. (1988). Studying writers' knowledge in academic disciplines. In D. Jolliffe (Ed.), *Writing in academic disciplines* (pp. 35–88). Norwood NJ: Ablex.

Kalmbach, J., & Gorman, M. E. (1986). Surveying classroom practices: How teachers teach writing. In A. Young & T. Fulwiler (Eds.), *Writing across the disciplines: Research into practice* (pp. 68–85). Portsmouth, NH: Boynton/Cook.

Kaufman, W. (1967). English does not belong to the English class. *English Journal, 56*(6), 269–270.

Keller, E. F. (1983). *A feeling for the organism.* San Francisco: Freeman.

Keller, E. F. (1985). *Reflections on gender and science.* New Haven: Yale University Press.

Kelly, G. J., & Bazerman, C. (2003). How Students Argue Scientific Claims: A Rhetorical-Semantic Analysis. *Applied Linguistics, 24*(1), 28–55.

Kelly, G. J., & Takao, A. (2002). Epistemic levels in argument: An analysis of university oceanography students' use of evidence in writing. *Science Education, 86,* 314–342.

Kemp, F. (1987). *Freeing the student voice: Establishing discourse communities through networked computers.* Penn State Conference on Rhetoric and Composition. State College, PA.

Kennedy, M. L. (1986). *Academic writing: Working with sources across the curriculum.* Englewood Cliffs, NJ: Prentice-Hall.

Keys, C. W. (1999). Revitalizing instruction in scientific genres: Connecting knowledge production with writing to learn in science. *Science Education, 83,* 115–130.

Keys, C. W. (2000). Investigating the thinking processes of eighth grade writers during the composition of a scientific laboratory report. *Journal of Research in Science Teaching, 37,* 676–690.

Keys, C. W., Hand, B., Prain, V., & Collins, S. (1999). Using the scientific writing heuristic as a tool for learning from laboratory investigations in secondary science. *Journal of Research in Science Teaching, 36,* 1065–1084.

Kinkead, J. (1997). Documenting excellence in teaching and learning in WAC programs. In K. B. Yancey & B. Huot (Eds.), *Assessing writing across the curriculum: Diverse approaches and practices* (pp. 37–50). Greenwich, CT: Ablex.

Kipling, K. J., & Murphy, R. J. (1992). *Symbiosis: Writing and an academic culture.* Portsmouth, NH: Boynton/Cook.

Kirsch, G. (1988). Students' interpretations of writing tasks: A case study. *Journal of Basic Writing, 7*(2), 81–90.

Klamer, A. (1984). *Conversations with economists: New classical economists and their opponents speak out on the current controversy in macroeconomics.* Totowa, NJ: Rowman & Allenheld.

Klamer, A. (1990). The textbook presentation of economic discourse. In W. J. Samuels (Ed.), *Economics as discourse* (pp. 129–154). Norwell, MA: Kluwer.

Klamer, A., & McCloskey, D. (1995). One-quarter of GDP is persuasion. *American Economic Review, 92,* 191–195.

Knorr-Cetina, K. (1979). Tinkering toward success: Prelude to a theory of scientific practice. *Theory and Society 8,* 347–376

Knorr-Cetina, K. (1981). *The manufacture of knowledge*. Oxford: Pergamon Press.

Kress, G. (1987). Genre in a social theory of language: A reply to John Dixon. In I. Reid (Ed.), *The place of genre in learning: Current debates* (pp. 25–45). Geelong, Australia: Deakin University Press.

Kristeva, J. (1980). *Desire in language: A semiotic approach to literature and art*. New York: Columbia University Press.

Kuhn, T. (1962). *The structure of scientific revolutions*. Chicago: University of Chicago Press.

Kuhn, T. S. (1961). The function of measurement in modern physical science. In H. Woolf (Ed.), *Quantification: A history of the meaning of measurement in the natural and social sciences* (pp. 31–63). Indianapolis, IN: Bobbs-Merrill.

Kuhn, T. S. (1996). *The structure of scientific revolutions* (3rd ed.). Chicago: University of Chicago Press.

Kulhavy, R., Dyer, J., & Silver, L. (1975). The effects of notetaking and test expectancy on the learning of text material. *Journal of Educational Research, 68*, 363–365.

Langer, J., & Applebee, A. (1987). *How writing shapes thinking: A study of teaching and learning*. Urbana, IL: NCTE.

Latour, B. (1987). *Science in action: How to follow scientists and engineers through society*. Cambridge, MA: Harvard University Press.

Latour, B., & Woolgar, S. (1979). *Laboratory life: The social construction of scientific facts*. Beverly Hills, CA: Sage.

LeBlanc, P. J. (1994). The politics of literacy and technology in secondary school classrooms. In C. L. Selfe & S. Hilligoss (Eds.), *Literacy and computers: The complications of teaching and learning with technology* (pp. 22–36). New York: MLA.

LeCourt, D. (1996). WAC as critical pedagogy: The third stage? *JAC: A Journal of Composition Theory, 16*, 389–405.

Leki, I. (2004). Meaning and development of academic literacy in a second language. In B. Huot, B. Stroble, & C. Bazerman (Eds.), *Multiple literacies for the 21ˢᵗ century* (pp. 115–128). Cresskill, NJ: Hampton.

Leontiev, A. N. (1978). *Activity, consciousness, and personality*. Englewood Cliffs, NJ: Prentice Hall.

Lévi-Strauss, C. (1975). *The raw and the cooked: Introduction to a science of mythology*. New York: Harper Colophon Books.

Li, X. M. (1996). *Good writing in cross-cultural context*. Albany, NY: SUNY Press.

Locke, D. M. (1992). *Science as writing*. New Haven: Yale University Press.

Lynch, M., & Woolgar, S. (Eds.). (1990). *Representation in scientific practice*. Cambridge, MA: MIT Press.

MacDonald, S. P. (1994). *Professional academic writing in the humanities and social sciences.* Carbondale: Southern Illinois University Press.

MacDonald, S. P., & Cooper, Charles M. (1992). Contributions of academic and dialogic journals to writing about literature. In A. Herrington & C. Moran (Eds.), *Writing, teaching, and learning in the disciplines* (pp. 137–155). New York: MLA.

McCarthy, L. P. (1987). A stranger in strange lands: A college student writing across the curriculum. *Research in the Teaching of English, 21,* 233–365.

McCarthy, L. P. (1991). A psychiatrist using DSM-III: The influence of a charter document in psychiatry. In C. Bazerman & J. Paradis (Eds.), *Textual dynamics of the professions* (pp. 358–378). Madison: University of Wisconsin Press.

McCarthy, L. P., & Fishman S. M. (1991). Boundary conversations: Conflicting ways of knowing in philosophy and interdisciplinary research. *Research in the Teaching of English, 25*(4), 419–468.

McCarthy, L. P., & Fishman, S. M. (1996). Culture on the page: Experience, rhetoric, and aesthetics in ethnographic writing. In P. Mortensen, & G. E. Kirsch (Eds.), *Ethics and representation in qualitative studies of literacy* (pp. 177–201). Urbana, IL: NCTE.

McCarthy, L. P., & Gerring, J. P. (1994). Revising psychiatry's charter document, DSM IV. *Written Communication, 11*(2), 147–192.

McCloskey, D. N. (1985). *The rhetoric of economics.* Madison, WI: University of Wisconsin Press.

McCloskey, D. N. (1990). *If you're so smart: The narrative of economic expertise.* Chicago: University of Chicago Press.

McCloskey, D. N. (1994). *Knowledge and persuasion in economics.* Cambridge: Cambridge University Press.

McCloskey, D. N. (1996). *The vices of economists, the virtues of the bourgeoisie.* Amsterdam: Amsterdam University Press.

McCrary, D. (2001). Womanist theology and its efficacy for the writing classroom. *College Composition and Communication, 52*(4), 521–552.

McCullogh, N. V. (1960). College wide English improvement. *College English, 21*(7), 407–408.

McElroy, J. L. (1997). The mentor demonstration model: Writing with students in senior economics seminar. *The Journal of Economic Education, 28*(1), 31–35.

McLeod, S. (Ed.). (1988). *Strengthening programs for writing across the curriculum.* San Francisco: Jossey-Bass.

McLeod, S. (1989). Writing across the curriculum: The second stage, and beyond. *College Composition and Communication, 40,* 337–343.

McLeod, S. (1992). WAC: An introduction. In S. McLeod & M. Soven (Eds.), *Writing across the curriculum: A guide to developing programs.* Newbury Park, CA: Sage Publications.

McLeod, S., & Maimon, E. (2000). Clearing the air: WAC myths and realities. *College English, 62*(5), 573–583.

McLeod, S., Miraglia, E., Soven, M., & Thaiss, C. (Eds.). (2001). *WAC for the new millennium: Strategies for continuing writing-across-the-curriculum programs.* Urbana, IL: NCTE.

McLeod, S. & Soven, M. (Eds.). (1992). *Writing across the curriculum: A guide to developing programs.* Newbury Park, CA: Sage Publications.

Mageau, T. (1990, November-December). Teaching and learning online. *Electronic Learning,* 26–30.

Mahala, D. (1991). Writing utopias: Writing across the curriculum and the promise of reform. *College English, 53*(7), 773–789.

Maimon, E. (1982). WAC: Past, present and future. In C. W. Griffin (Ed.), *Teaching writing in all disciplines.* San Francisco: Jossey-Bass.

Maimon, E. (1981). *Writing in the arts and sciences.* Boston: Little, Brown.

Maki, U. (1988). How to combine rhetoric and realism in the methodology of economics. *Economics and Philosophy, 4,* 89–109.

Marcus, G. (1995). Ethnography in/of the world system: The emergence of multi-sited ethnography. *Annual Review of Anthropology, 24,* 95–117.

Marcus, G. E. (1980a). The ethnographic subject as ethnographer: A neglected dimension of anthropological research. *Rice University Studies, 66*(1), 55–68.

Marcus, G. E. (1980b). Rhetoric and the ethnographic genre in anthropological research. *Current Anthropology, 21,* 507–510.

Marcus, G. E., & Clifford, J. (1985). The making of ethnographic texts: A preliminary report. *Current Anthropology, 26,* 267–271.

Marcus, G. E., & Cushman, D. (1982). Ethnographies as texts. *Annual Review of Anthropology, 11,* 25–69.

Marland, M. (1977). *Language across the curriculum: The implementation of the Bullock Report in the secondary school.* London: Heinemann Educational Books.

Marsella, J., Hilgers, T. L., & McLaren, C. (1992). How students handle writing assignments: A study of eighteen responses in six disciplines. In A. Herrington & C. Moran (Eds.), *Writing, teaching and learning in the disciplines* (pp. 174–188). New York: Modern Language Associates.

Martin, J. R. (1992). English text: system and structure. Philadelphia: John Benjamin's Publishing Company.

Martin, J., Christie, F., & Rothery, J. (1987). Social processes in education: A reply to Sawyer and Watson (and others). In I. Reid (Ed.), *The place of genre in learning; Current debates* (pp. 55–58). Geelong, Australia: Deakin University Press.

Martin, N. (1976). *Writing and learning across the curriculum.* London: Ward Lock Educational.

Martin, N. (Ed.). (1984). *Writing across the curriculum pamphlets: a selection from the schools council and London University Institute of Education joint project.* Upper Montclair, NJ: Boynton/Cook.

Medawar, P. B. (1964). Is the scientific paper fraudulent? *Saturday Review, 1,* 42–43.

Medway, P. (2000). Writing and design in architectural education. In P. Dias &A. Paré (Eds.), *Transitions: Writing in academic and workplace settings* (pp. 89–128). Cresskill, NJ: Hampton Press,

Medway, P. (2002). Fuzzy genres and community identities: The case of architecture students' sketchbooks. In R. Coe, L. Lingard, & T. Teslenko (Eds.), *The rhetoric and ideology of genre: Strategies for stability and change* (pp. 123–154). Cresskill, NJ: Hampton Press.

Miller, C. (1984). Genre as social action. *Quarterly Journal of Speech, 70,* 151–167.

Miner, H. (1956). Body ritual among the Nacirema. *American Anthropologist, 58,* 503–507.

Moffett, J. (1968). *Teaching the universe of discourse.* Boston: Houghton Mifflin.

Moffett, J. (1981). *Active voice: A writing program across the curriculum.* Upper Montclair, NJ: Boynton/Cook..

Monaghan, E. J. (1989). Literacy and gender in colonial New England. In Cathy Davidson (Ed.), *Reading in America (*pp. 53–80). Baltimore: Johns Hopkins University Press.

Monroe, J. (Ed.). (2002). *Writing and revising the disciplines.* Ithaca, NY: Cornell University Press.

Montgomery, S. (1996). *The scientific voice.* New York: Guilford Press.

Morgan, M. (1997). The crazy quilt of writing across the curriculum: Achieving WAC program assessment. In K. B. Yancey & B. Huot (Eds.), *Assessing writing across the curriculum: Diverse approaches and practices* (pp. 141–158). Greenwich, CT: Ablex.

Moss, A., & Holder, C. (1988) *Improving student writing: A guidebook for faculty in all disciplines.* Dubuque, IA: Kendall Hunt.

Moulthrop, S., & Kaplan, N. (1994). They became what they beheld: The futility of resistance in the space of electronic writing. In C. L. Selfe & S. Hilligoss (Eds.), *Literacy and computers: The complications of teaching and learning with technology* (pp. 220–237). New York: MLA.

Mulkay, M. (1985). *The word and the world.* London: George Allen & Unwin.

Mullin, J. (2001). Writing centers and WAC. In McCleod, et al. (Eds.), *WAC for the new millenium* (pp. 179–199). Urbana IL: NCTE.

Murray, D. M. (1991). *The craft of revision.* Fort Worth: Holt, Rinehart, and Winston.

Myers, G. (1989). The pragmatics of politeness in scientific articles. *Applied Linguistics, 10,* 1–35.

Myers, G. (1990a). *Writing biology: Texts in the social construction of scientific knowledge.* Madison: University of Wisconsin Press.

Myers, G. (1990b). The rhetoric of irony in academic writing. *Written Communication, 7,* 419–455

Myers, G. (1991). Stories and styles in two molecular biology articles. In C. Bazerman & J. Paradis (Eds.), *Textual dynamics of the professions* (pp. 45–75). Madison: University of Wisconsin Press.

Myers, J. W. (1984). *Writing to learn across the curriculum.* Bloomington, IN: Phi Delta Kappa Educational Foundation.

Nelson, J. (1990). This was an easy assignment: Examining how students interpret academic writing tasks. *Research in the Teaching of English, 24*(4), 362–396.

Nelson, J. S., Megill, A., & McCloskey, D. N. (Eds.). (1987). *The rhetoric of the human sciences: Language and argument in scholarship and public affairs.* Madison, WI: University of Wisconsin Press.

Newell, G. (1984). Learning from writing in two content areas: A case study/ protocol analysis. *Research in the Teaching of English, 18,* 265–287.

Newell, G., & Winograd, P. (1989). The effects of writing on learning from expository text. *Written Communication, 6,* 196–217.

Nystrand, M. (1990). Sharing words: The effects of readers on developing writers. *Written Communication, 7*(1), 3–24.

Nystrand, M., & Gamoran, A. (1991). Instructional discourse, student engagement, and literature achievement . *Research in the Teaching of English, 25*(3), 261–290.

Overington, M. A. (1977). The scientific community as audience: Toward a rhetorical analysis of science. *Journal of Philosophy and Rhetoric, 10*(3), 143–163.

Palmini, D. J. (1996). Using rhetorical cases to teach writing skills and enhance economic learning. *The Journal of Economic Education, 27*(3), 205–216.

Pennebaker, J. W., & Beall, S. K. (1986). Confronting a traumatic event: Toward an understanding of inhibition and disease. *Journal of Abnormal Psychology, 95,* 274–281.

Pera, M. (1994). *The discourses of science.* Chicago: University of Chicago Press.

Pera, M., & Shea, W. (Eds.). (1991). *Persuading science: The art of scientific rhetoric.* Canton, MA: Science History Publishers.

Petraglia, J. (Ed.). (1995). *Reconceiving writing, rethinking writing instruction.* Mahwah, NJ: Erlbaum.

Porter, J. (1986). Intertextuality and the discourse community. *Rhetoric Review, 5,* 34–47.

Potter, J., & Wetherell, M. (1987). *Discourse and social psychology.* Beverly Hills, CA: Sage.

Prain, V., & Hand, B. (1999). Students perceptions of writing for learning in secondary school science. *Science Education, 83,* 151–162.

Prelli, L. J. (1989). *A rhetoric of science: inventing scientific discourse.* Columbia, SC: University of South Carolina Press.

Prior, P. A. (1998). *Writing/disciplinarity: A sociohistoric account of literate activity in the academy.* Mahwah, NJ: Erlbaum.

Purves, A. (Ed.). (1988*). Writing across languages and cultures: Issues in contrastive rhetoric.* Newbury Park, CA: Sage.

Rabinor, J. R. (1991). The process of recovery from an eating disorder: The use of journal writing in the initial phase of treatment. *Psychotherapy in Private Practice, 9,* 93–106.

Radmacher, S. A., & Latosi-Sawin, E. (1995). Summary writing: A tool to improve student comprehension and writing in psychology. *Teaching of Psychology, 22*(2), 113–115.

Reid, I. (Ed.). (1987). *The place of genre in learning: Current debates.* Geelong, Australia: Deakin University Press.

Reisch, C. (2000). Teaching exchange: Introduction to math autobiography and course reflection assignments. *Academic Writing.* Available: http://wac.colostate.edu/aw/teaching/reisch2000/index.htm

Reiss, D., Selfe, D., & Young, A. (Eds.). (1998). *Electronic communication across the curriculum.* Urbana, IL: NCTE.

Reynolds, J. F., Mair, David, C., & Fischer, P. C. (1992). *Writing and reading mental health records.* Newbury Park, CA: Sage.

Richards, I. A. (1936). *The philosophy of rhetoric.* New York: Oxford University Press.

Risemberg, R. (1996). Reading to write: Self-regulated learning strategies when writing essays from sources. *Reading Research and Instruction, 35*(4), 365–383.

Rivard, L. P., & Straw, S. B. (2000). The effect of talk and writing on learning science: An exploratory study. *Science Education, 84,* 566–593.

Rosaldo, R. (1980). *Ilongot headhunting, 1883–1974: A study in society and history.* Stanford, CA: Stanford University Press.

Rosaldo, R. (1987). Where objectivity lies: the rhetoric of anthropology. In J. S. Nelson, A. Megill, & D. N. McCloskey (Eds.), *The rhetoric of the human sciences* (pp. 87–110). Madison, WI: University of Wisconsin Press.

Rosenberg, A. (1988). Economics is too important to be left to the rhetoricians. *Economics and Philosophy, 4,* 129–149.

Rossetti, J. (1990). Deconstructing Robert Lucas. In W. J. Samuels (Ed.), *Economics as discourse* (pp. 225–243). Norwell, MA: Kluwer.

Roth, P. (1989). Ethnography without tears. *Current Anthropology, 30*(5), 555–561.

Rudd, J.A, Greenbowe, T.J., & Hand, B. (2001). Reshaping the general chemistry laboratory report using the science writing heuristic. *Journal of College Science Teaching, 31,* 230–234.

Rudd, J. A., Greenbowe, T.J., Hand, B.M., & Legg, M.L. (2001). Using the science writing heuristic to move toward an inquiry-based laboratory curriculum: An example from physical equilibrium. *Journal of Chemical Education, 78,* 1680–1686.

Russell, D. R. (1988). Romantics on writing: Liberal culture and the abolition of composition courses. *Rhetoric Review, 6*(2), 132–148.

Russell, D. R. (1991). *Writing in the academic disciplines, 1870–1990: A curricular history.* Carbondale, IL: Southern Illinois University Press.

Russell, D. R. (1994). American origins of the writing-across-the-curriculum movement. In C. Bazerman & D. Russell (Eds.), *Landmark essays on writing across the curriculum* (pp. 3–22). Davis, CA: Hermagoras Press.

Russell, D. R. (1997a). Rethinking genre in school and society: An activity theory analysis. *Written Communication, 14,* 504–554.

Russell, D. R. (1997b). Writing and genre in higher education and workplaces. *Mind, Culture, and Activity, 4*(4), 224–237.

Russell, D. R. (2001). Where do the naturalistic studies of WAC/WID point to? In S. McLeod, E. Miraglia, M. Soven, & C. Thaiss (Eds.). (2001). *WAC for the new millennium: Strategies for continuing writing-across-the-curriculum programs* (pp. 259–298). Urbana, IL: NCTE.

Samuels, W. J. (1990). Introduction. In W. J. Samuels (Ed.), *Economics as discourse* (pp. 1–14). Norwell, MA: Kluwer.

Sanjek, R. (Ed.). (1990). *Fieldnotes: The making of anthropology.* Ithica, NY: Cornell University Press.

Sapir, E. (1949). *Selected writings in language, culture and personality.* Berkeley: University of California Press.

Scarcella, R. (2003). Academic English: A conceptual framework. (Technical Report, Linguistic Minority Research Institute, University of California) 2003–1.

Schaffer, S. (1994). Self evidence. In J. Chandler, A. Davis, & H. Harootunian, (Eds.), *Questions of evidence: Proof, practice, and persuasion across the disciplines.* Chicago: University of Chicago Press.

Schön, D. A. (1983). *The reflective practitioner: How professionals think in action.* New York: Basic Books.

Schrum, L. (1988, October). Telecommunications: A window to the world. *Instructor,* 31–32.

Schryer, C. F., Lingard, L., Spafford, M., & Garwood, K. (2003). Structure and Agency in Medical Case Presentations. In C. Bazerman and D. R. Russell (Eds.), *Writing selves/writing societies: Research from activity Perspectives: Perspectives on writing.* Fort Collins, CO: The WAC Clear-

inghouse. [On-line]. Available: http://wac.colostate.edu/books/selves_
societies/

Schultz, C., & di Vesta, F. (1972). Effects of passage organization and note
taking on the selection of clustering strategies and on recall of textual
materials. *Journal of Educational Psychology, 63,* 244–252.

Schutz, A. (1967). *The problem of social reality.* The Hague: Martinus Ni-
jhoff.

Schutz, A., & Luckmann, T. (1973). *The structures of the life-world.* Evan-
ston, IL: Northwestern University Press.

Schwartz, H. J. (1984). Teaching writing with computer aids. *College English,*
46(3), 239–247.

Schwartz, H. J. (1982). Monsters and mentors: Computer applications for
humanistic education. *College English, 44*(2), 141–152.

Schwegler, R., & Shamoon, L. (1991). Meaning attribution in ambiguous
texts. In C. Bazerman & J. Paradis (Eds.), *Textual dynamics of the profes-*
sions (pp. 216–34). Madison: University of Wisconsin Press.

Scully, M. G. (1974, September 23). Crisis in English writing. *Chronicle of*
Higher Education. 1.

Selfe, C. (1997). Contextual evaluation in WAC programs. In K. B. Yancey,
& B. Huot (Eds.). *Assessing writing across the curriculum: Diverse ap-*
proaches and practices. (pp. 51–68). Greenwich, CT: Ablex.

Selfe, C., & Arbabi, F. (1983). Writing to learn: Engineering student journals. *Engineering Education, 74,* 86–90.

Selfe, C., & Arbabi, F. (1986). Writing to learn: Engineering student journals. In A.Young, & T. Fulwiler (Eds.), *Writing across the disciplines: Re-*
search into practice (pp. 184–191) Upper Montclair, NJ: Boynton/Cook.

Selzer, J. (Ed.). (1993a). *Understanding Scientific Prose.* Madison: University
of Wisconsin Press.

Selzer, J. (1993b). Intertextuality and the writing process. In R. Spilka (Ed.),
Writing in the workplace (pp. 171–180). Carbondale: Southern Illinois
University Press.

Semas, P. W. (1975, November 3). The explosion of growth of 'faculty development'. *Chronicle of Higher Education, 3.*

Sgoutas-Emch, S. A., & Johnson, C. J. (1998). Is journal writing an effective method of reducing anxiety towards statistics? *Journal of Instructional*
Psychology, 25, 49–57.

Shapin, S. (1994*). A social history of truth: Civility and science in seventeenth-*
century England. Chicago: University of Chicago Press.

Shapin, S., & Schaffer, S. (1985). *Leviathan and the air-pump: Hobbes, Boyle*
and the experimental life. Princeton: Princeton University Press.

Shea, W. (1972). *Galileo's intellectual revolution.* London: Macmillan.

Siegfried, J. J., Bartlett, R., Hansen, W. L., Kelley, A. C., McCloskey, D. N., & Tietenberg, T. H. (1991). The status and prospects of the economics major. *Journal of Economic Education, 22*(3), 197–224

Simons, H. (1990). The rhetoric of inquiry as an intellectual movement. In H. Simons (Ed.), *The rhetorical turn: Invention and persuasion in the conduct of inquiry* (pp. 1–31). Chicago: University of Chicago Press.

Simpson, M. S., & Carroll, S. E. (1999). Assignments for a writing-intensive economics course. *Journal of Economic Education, 30*(4), 402–410.

Sipple, J. M.(1987). Teacher protocols: A new evaluation tool for writing across the curriculum programs. (ERIC Document Reproduction Service No. ED 285 150).

Siskin, L. S., & Little, J. (1995). *The subjects in question: Departmental organization and the high school.* New York: Teachers College Press.

Slaughter, M. M. (1985*). Universal languages and scientific taxonomy in the seventeenth century.* Princeton, NJ: Princeton University Press.

Small, H. (1978). Cited documents as concept symbols. *Social Studies of Science, 8,* 327–340.

Smart, G. (1993). Genre as community invention. In R. Spilka (Ed.), *Writing in the workplace* (pp. 124–140). Carbondale: Southern Illinois University Press.

Smart, G. (1999). Storytelling in a central bank: The role of narrative in the creation and use of specialized economic knowledge. *Journal of Business and Technical Communication 13,* 249–273.

Smart, G. (2000). Reinventing expertise: Experienced writers in the workplace encounter a new genre. In P. Dias & A. Paré (Eds.), *Transitions: Writing in academic and workplace settings* (pp. 223–252). Cresskill, NJ: Hampton Press.

Smart, G. (2002). A central bank's communications strategy: The interplay of activity, discourse genres, and technology in a time of organizational change. In C. Bazerman & D. Russell (Eds.), *Writing selves/writing societies: Research from activity perspectives: Perspectives on writing.* Fort Collins, CO: The WAC Clearinghouse. [On-line]. Available: http://wac.colostate.edu/books/selves_societies/

Smithson, I., & Sorrentino, P. (1987). Writing across the curriculum: An assessment. *Journal of Teaching Writing, 6*(2), 325–342.

Snodgrass, S. E. (1985). Writing as a tool for teaching social psychology. *Teaching of Psychology, 12*(2), 91–94.

Song, B., & Richter, E. (1997). Tutoring in the classroom: A quantitative study. *Writing Center Journal, 18*(1), 50–60.

Soven, M. (1996). *Write to learn: A guide to writing across the curriculum.* Cincinnati, OH: South Western College Pub.

Soven, M. (2001). Curriculum-based peer tutors and WAC. In McCleod, et al. (Eds.), *WAC for the new millenium* (pp. 200–232). Urbana IL: NCTE.

Soven, M., & McLeod, S. (Eds.). (in press*). Creating A Community: The Beginnings of the WAC Movement* . West Lafayette, IN: Parlor Press.

Soyland, A. J. (1994). *Psychology as Metaphor.* London: Sage.

Spencer, J. (1989). Anthropology as a Kind of Writing. *Man, 24,* 145–64.

Spivey, N. N. (1990). Transforming texts: Constructive processes in reading and writing. *Written Communication, 7*(2), 256–287.

Sprague, R. K. (1972). *The older Sophists.* Columbia, SC: University of South Carolina Press.

Steering Committee (2001). WPA Outcomes Statement for First-Year Composition. *College English, 63*(3), 321–325.

Steffens, H. (1989). Designing history writing assignments for student success. *Social Studies, 80*(2), 59–63.

Stewart, L. R. (1992). *The rise of public science: Rhetoric, technology, and natural philosophy in Newtonian Britain, 1660–1750.* Cambridge, England: Cambridge University Press.

Stigler, G. (1982). *The economist as preacher and other essays.* Chicago: University of Chicago Press.

Sutton, M. (1978). The writing adjunct program at the small college of California State University, Dominguez Hills. In J. Neel (Ed.), *Options for the teaching of English: Freshman composition* (pp. 104–109). New York: MLA.

Swales, J. (1990). *Genre analysis: English in academic and research settings.* Cambridge: Cambridge University Press.

Swales, J. (1998). *Other floors, other voices: A textography of a small university building.* Mahwah, NJ: Erlbaum.

Swales, J. M., & Feak, C. B. (2000). *English in today's research world: A writing guide.* Ann Arbor, MI: University of Michigan Press.

Swilky, J. (1992). Reconsidering faculty resistance to writing reform. *Writing Program Administration, 16*(1–2), 50–61.

Tanner, D., & Tanner, L. (1990). *History of the school curriculum.* New York: Macmillan.

Taylor, R. (1980). *The computer in the school: Tutor, tool, and tutee.* New York: Teachers College Press.

Tchudi, S. (1986). *Teaching writing in the content areas: College level.* Washington, DC: National Education Association of the United States

Tchudi, S., & Tchudi, S. J. (1983). *Teaching writing in the content areas: Elementary school.* Washington, DC: National Education Association.

Tchudi, S. N., & Huerta, M. C. (1983). *Teaching writing in the content areas: Middle school/junior high.* Washington, DC: National Education Association,

Tchudi, S. N., & Yates, J. (1983). *Teaching writing in the content areas: Senior high school.* Washington, DC: NEA Professional Library.

Thaiss, C. J. (1986). *Language across the curriculum in the elementary grades.* Urbana, IL: NCTE.

Thaiss, C. J., & Suhor, C. (Eds.). (1984). *Speaking and writing, K-12: Classroom strategies and the new research.* Urbana, IL: NCTE.

Thornton, T. P. (1996). *Handwriting in America.* New Haven: Yale University Press.

Tobey, D. M. (1979). Writing instruction in economic courses: Experimentation across disciplines. *Journal of Northeastern Agricultural Economics Council, 8,* 159–164.

Townsend, M. (2001). Writing intensive courses and WAC. In McCleod, et al. (Eds.), *WAC for the new millenium* (pp. 233–258). Urbana IL: NCTE.

Traweek, S. (1988). *Beamtimes and lifetimes.* Cambridge, MA: MIT Press.

Treichler, P. (2000). *How to have theory in an epidemic: Cultural chronicles of AIDS.* Duke University Press.

Treichler, P., Cartwright, L., & Penley, C. (Eds.). *The visible woman: Imaging technologies, gender, and science.* New York: New York University Press, 1998.

Tuana, N. (Ed.). (1989). *Feminism & science.* Bloomington, IN: Indiana University Press.

Van Maanen, J. (Ed.). (1988). *Tales of the field: On writing ethnography.* Chicago: University of Chicago Press.

Van Maanen, J. (Ed.). (1995). Representation in ethnography. Thousand Oaks: Sage.

Van Nostrand, A. D. (1997). *Fundable knowledge.* Mahwah, NJ: Erlbaum.

VanSledright, B.A., & Frankes, L. (1998). Literature's place in learning history and science. In C. Hynd (Ed.), *Learning from text: Views across conceptual domains* (pp. 117–138). Hillsdale, NJ: Erlbaum.

Villanueva, V. (2001). The politics of literacy across the curriculum. In McLeod, et al. (Eds.), *WAC for the new millenium* (pp. 165–178). Urbana IL: NCTE.

Vipond, D. (1993a). Social motives for writing Psychology: Writing for and with younger readers. *Teaching of Psychology, 20,* 89–93.

Vipond, D. (1993b). *Writing and psychology: Understanding writing and its teaching from the perspective of composition studies.* Westport, CN: Praeger.

Voelker, J. C. (1978, November). Literacy as disease. *Chronicle of Higher Education,* p. 18.

Volosinov, V. N. (1986). *Marxism and the philosophy of language.* Cambridge MA: Harvard University Press.

Vygotsky, L. S. (1962). *Thought and language.* (E. Hanfmann & G. Vakar, Eds. & Trans.). Cambridge: MIT Press.

Vygotsky, L. S. (1978). *Mind in Society.* Cambridge: Harvard University Press.

Vygotsky, L. S. (1986). *Thought and language* (Alex Kozulin, Trans.). Cambridge: MIT Press.

Waldo, Mark L. (2004). *Demythologizing language difference in the academy: Establishing discipline-based writing programs.* Mahwah, NJ: Erlbaum.

Walvoord, B. (1982). *Helping students write well: A guide for teachers in all disciplines.* NewYork: Modern Language Association of America.

Walvoord, B. (1997). From conduit to consumer: The role of WAC faculty in WAC assessment. In K. B. Yancey, & B. Huot (Eds.). *Assessing writing across the curriculum: Diverse approaches and practices* (pp. 15–36). Greenwich, CT: Ablex Pub.Corp.

Walvoord, B., Hunt, L. L., Dowling, H. F., & McMahon, J. D. (1997). *In the long run: A study of faculty in three writing-across-the-curriculum programs.* Urbana, IL: NCTE.

Walvoord, B., & McCarthy, L. (1990). *Thinking and writing in college: A naturalistic study of students in four disciplines.* Urbana, IL: NCTE.

Weimer, W. (1977). Science as a rhetorical transaction: Toward a non-justificational conception of rhetoric. *Philosophy and Rhetoric, 10,* 1–29.

Weintraub, E. R. (2002). *How economics became a mathematical science.* Durham, NC: Duke University Press.

Williamson, M. M. (1997). Pragmatism, positivism, and program evaluation. In K. B. Yancey & B. Huot (Eds.), *Assessing writing across the curriculum: Diverse approaches and practices* (pp. 237–258). Greenwich, CT: Ablex.

Winograd, K. (1993). Selected writing behaviors of fifth graders as they composed original mathematics story problems. *Research in the Teaching of English, 27*(4), 369–394.

Winsor, D. A. (1996). *Writing like an engineer: A rhetorical education.* Mahwah, NJ: Erlbaum.

Winsor, D. A. (2003). *Writing power: Communication in an engineering center.* Albany: State University of New York Press.

Wollman-Bonilla, J. E. (1998). Teaching science writing to first graders: Genre learning and recontextualization. *Research in the Teaching of English, 33*(2), 158–180.

Woolgar, S. (1981). Discovery: Logic and sequence in a scientific text. In K. Knorr, R. Krohn, & R. Whitley (Eds.), *The social processes of scientific discovery* (pp. 239–68). Dordrecht, Netherlands: Reidel.

Woolgar, S. (Ed.). (1988). *Knowledge and reflexivity: New frontiers in the sociology of knowledge.* London: Sage.

Wright, H. B.(1949). Faculty responsibility for student writing. *College English* 11,160–161.

Wyatt, F. (2001). Publishing biographies to learn about history, writing, and research. *Middle School Journal, 32*(5), 7–12.

Yancey, K. B., & Huot, B. (Eds.). (1997). *Assessing writing across the curriculum: Diverse approaches and practices.* Greenwich, CT: Ablex.

Yearley, S. (1981). Textual persuasion: The role of scientific accounting in the construction of scientific arguments. *Philosophy of the Social Sciences, 11,* 409–435.

Young, A., & Fulwiler, T. (1986). *Writing across the disciplines: Research into practice.* Upper Montclair. NJ: Boynton/Cook.

Young, K. M., & Leinhardt, G. (1998). Writing from primary documents: A way of knowing in history. *Written Communication, 15*(1), 25–68.

Zamel, V. (1995). Strangers in academia: The experiences of faculty and ESL students across the curriculum. *College Composition and Communication, 46,* 506–521.

Zamel, V. (1998). Questioning academic discourse. In V. Zamel & R. Spack (Eds.), *Negotiating academic literacies: Teaching and learning across languages and cultures* (pp. 187–198). Mahwah, NJ: Erlbaum.

Zawacki, T. M., & Williams, A. W. (2001). Writing within interdisciplinary learning communities. In McLeod, et al. (Eds.), *WAC for the new millenium* (pp. 179–199). Urbana IL: NCTE.

Zlotkowski, E. (1998). A new model for excellence. In E. Zlotkowski (Ed.), *Successful service-learning programs: New models of excellence in higher education.* (pp. 1–14). Bolton, MA: Anker.

About the Authors

Charles Bazerman, Professor and Chair of the Department of Education at the University of California, Santa Barbara, is interested in the social dynamics of writing, rhetorical theory, and the rhetoric of knowledge production and use. He has been active in developing graduate degree objectives in rhetoric, literacy, and communication at UCSB and previously at Georgia Tech. His most recent books are a collection of essays co-edited with David Russell on writing and activity theory, *Writing Selves and Societies*, (available online at http://wac.colostate.edu/books/selves_societies/) and a methods book on textual analysis co-edited with Paul Prior, *What Writing Does and How It Does It*. His book, *The Languages of Edison's Light*, won the Association of American Publisher's award for the best scholarly book of 1999 in the History of Science and Technology. Previous books include *Constructing Experience, Shaping Written Knowledge: The Genre and Activity of the Experimental Article in Science, The Informed Writer: Using Sources in the Disciplines*, and *Involved: Writing For College, Writing for Your Self*. Co-edited volumes include *Textual Dynamics of the Professions, Landmark Essays in Writing Across the Curriculum*, and a special issue of *Mind, Culture, Activity* on "The Activity of Writing, The Writing of Activity." Current projects include a rhetorical theory of literate action, an investigation of environmental information, examination of writing in a geology course, and an investigation of tensions among writing assessment devices. He is also editing the *Handbook of Writing Research* and is editor of the Reference Guides to Rhetoric and Composition for Parlor Press.

Lisa Bethel teaches writing in the Los Angeles area.

Teri Chavkin is a Doctoral student in the Gevirtz Graduate School of Education, University of California, Santa Barbara, specializing in the teaching of writing. Her research focuses on writing processes of students with High Functioning Autism.

Danielle Fouquette is Instructor of English at Fullerton College, where she teaches writing. Her research interests concern the assumptions and perspectives that lie behind teacher comments on student papers and how students interpret and understand those comments.

Janet Garufis is adding graduate studies in writing to a successful career in the banking industry. Her interests include business writing, writing and identity, and social justice.

Joseph Little is a writer and teacher of writing who lives and works in Toronto. He studied writing at the University of Minnesota and at the University of California, Santa Barbara, where he received his PhD in Language, Literacy, and Composition Studies in 2004. Little's research and teaching interests surround disciplinary writing practices, technical writing, and personal writing. His work has been published in *Written Communication, Rhetoric Society Quarterly,* and the *Journal of Technical Writing and Communication.*

Index

academic language, 47
Academic.Writing, 24
Across the Disciplines, 24, 130
activity theory, 83, 89, 90, 95, 96
admissions, 30
agency, 53, 78, 94, 98
alignment, 45, 47, 54, 82, 99
American Psychological Association, 81
anthropology, 67, 68, 123
anxiety, 64, 132
Applebee, Arthur, 58, 59, 60
Ars Dictaminis, 89
assessment, 21, 25–26, 40–41, 46–47, 49, 50, 57, 71, 85, 107, 120, 121–128, 133, 137–138
authority, 7, 8, 13, 63, 66, 67, 68, 70, 71, 75, 76, 101, 133, 136–137
authorship, 54, 117
Bakhtin, Mikhail, 40, 93, 96, 117
Barnes, Douglas, 20
Bay Area Writing Project, 28
Bazerman, Charles, 20, 55, 65, 73, 80, 81, 82, 83, 89, 90, 92–95, 97, 103, 121
Beaver College, 26, 27
Berkenkotter, Carol, 83, 95, 100
biology, 7, 10, 16, 45, 49, 51, 56, 62, 71, 74, 83, 91
Blakeslee, Ann, 53, 82, 95
Britain, 20, 21, 22, 57
Britton, James, 20, 21, 22, 27, 38, 57, 58, 60

Brooklyn College, 28
Bruffee, Kenneth, 28, 116–117
Bruner, Jerome S., 20
Bullock Report, 21
Burke, Kenneth, 69
business, 6, 10, 11, 15, 17, 22, 47, 50–51, 125
California State Dominguez Hills, 28
Carleton College, 23, 26, 110
Casanave, Chris, 54, 95, 99, 112–113
Central College, 26
Chronicle of Higher Education, 30, 31
citation, 12, 13, 72, 75, 80, 84
Clifford, James, 67, 68, 117
collaboration, 21, 27, 28, 51, 53, 114
College Composition and Communication, 23–24
communications movement, 19
composition, 8, 9, 16–18, 20, 25, 28, 45, 61, 86, 88, 90, 94, 100, 113–114, 116–118, 129–130, 134
CompPile, 130
computer, 62, 115–119
computer science, 62
Cornell University, 24, 28
Darwin, Charles, 77, 79
Dear, Peter, 76
democratization, 15, 18
Devitt, Amy, 91–92